SIXTEEN MINUTES FROM HOME

The Columbia Space Shuttle Tragedy

by
Mark Cantrell and Donald Vaughan

Edited by
Nicholas Maier

American Media Inc.

Sixteen Minutes from Home
The Columbia Space Shuttle Tragedy

Copyright © 2003 AMI Books, Inc.

Cover design: Jim Johnston
Interior design: Debbie Duckworth and Debbie Browning

ISBN: 1-932270-10-8

First printing: April 2003

Printed in the United States of America

10 9 8 7 6 5 4 3 2 1

Table of Contents

Authors' Note

Early on the morning of February 1, 2003, the space shuttle Columbia re-entered the Earth's atmosphere slightly south of California after a flawless 16-day mission. Over the next few minutes, Mission Control engineers watched with rising concern as the left wing's temperature sensors suddenly went out one by one. Three minutes later, other sensors on the left main landing gear also went dead. After a garbled radio transmission from Columbia, Mission Control asked Commander Rick Husband to repeat, and received what would be the final transmission from the ship: "Roger. Buh . . ."

Just minutes later, Columbia, the flagship of the shuttle fleet and a veteran of 28 successful missions, fell to Earth in charred pieces. Television viewers around the globe sat in anguish as video footage of the tragedy, captured by professional cameramen and amateurs alike, played over and over again. Although 17 years had passed since the Challenger exploded on a cold January morning in 1986, the memories of that awful day came rushing back, a shocking wake-up call to a world grown complacent by the seemingly routine nature of space travel.

But, as the astronauts and their families well knew, there is nothing routine about exploring the cosmos. The tragedy of Space Transportation System-107, or STS-107 as it was known in NASA jargon, immediately raised a host of questions. What caused the destruction of the 113th shuttle flight, and what impact would it have on NASA's shuttle program and space exploration in general? After the Challenger disaster, it took years for NASA to recover. What effect would the loss of Columbia have? Could anything have been done to save the astronauts?

Shortly before his death in 1963, President John F. Kennedy acknowledged that the road to space would not be easy or safe, saying: "We stand on the edge of a great new era, filled with both crisis and opportunity, an era to be characterized by achievement and by challenge. It is an era which calls for action and for the best efforts of all those who would test the unknown and the uncertain in every phase of human endeavor. It is a time for pathfinders and pioneers."

This book is dedicated to those space pioneers who died in the Texas skies that horrible day, as well as those who preceded them. They epitomized the best humanity has to offer, and embodied the adventurous spirit that has always made humans push the boundaries of what is possible. Despite the danger, they never turned away from that calling. In the months and years to come, there can be no greater tribute to their sacrifice than to continue their voyage of discovery.

Chapter 1
The Death of Columbia

"A space-shuttle contingency has been declared."

That simple sentence, spoken by the faceless voice of Mission Control in Houston and immediately reported on the official government NASA website, was the first public notice that something had gone horribly wrong during what was anticipated to be an uneventful, routine re-entry for the space shuttle Columbia on Saturday, February 1, 2003.

But as the world would quickly learn, the orbiter's return from its 16-day mission had gone from flawless to calamitous in a matter of moments. In the cloudless blue skies above the Texas plains, the shuttle seemed to explode with a series of thunderous booms and then literally fell to pieces, depositing flaming debris and the remains of its crew over a several-hundred-mile swath through mid-Texas and Louisiana. Days later, as more information came in, the debris field was extended as far west as California.

* * *

Their final day in space started extremely well for Columbia's tight-knit, seven-member crew. They were awakened to the strains of Scotland the Brave, performed by the 51st Highland Brigade, in honor of Mission Specialist Laurel Clark, who was of Scottish descent. A different song is played each morning, often one of significance to a particular crew member. The previous day the crew had awoken to Shalom Lach Eretz Nehederet in honor of Payload Specialist Ilan Ramon, a revered war hero in his native Israel and the first Israeli astronaut.

Mission Control greeted the astronauts that Saturday with a cheerful "good morning" and Clark answered: "Good morning, Houston. We're getting ready for our big day up here . . . I'm really excited to come back home. Hearing that song reminded me of all the different places down on Earth and all the friends and family that I have all over the world."

The chores of the morning, though relatively simple, were time consuming. After crawling out of the sleep supports that kept them stationary in zero gravity and downing a quick breakfast, they stowed their remaining equipment, a process that took nearly six hours. Their mission complete, they then fastened themselves into their seats, held firm by straps that were specially designed to protect them during the tricky maneuvering of re-entry. On the flight deck were Commander Rick Husband, Pilot William McCool, Mission Specialist Kalpana Chawla and Clark. Enjoying the loud, bumpy ride on the deck below were Ramon, Payload Commander Michael Anderson and Mission Specialist David Brown.

No one aboard the orbiter or at Mission Control in Houston had reason to believe that this re-entry would be any different from the previous 111 shuttle flights, 27 of which had been made by the 22-year-old Columbia, the first and perhaps the most stalwart of NASA's shuttle fleet. After all, nothing had ever gone wrong during a shuttle return — the only other disaster in the program's history, the destruction of the shuttle Challenger in January 1986, had occurred 73 seconds after liftoff.

Before that horrifying event, NASA had boldly claimed that the chances of a deadly shuttle accident were just 1 in 100,000. After Challenger, the risk ratio increased dramatically to 1 in 148. However, many NASA employees said anonymously that the risk is almost certainly even higher, perhaps 1 in 75. The reason is simple: space shuttles are astonishingly complicated vehicles with more than 2.5 million parts. The ships contain a wealth of failsafes, back-ups and systems checks, but it's virtually impossible to verify the integrity of every single component before each flight. Every member of NASA's astronaut corps — the unique men and women who possess what writer Tom Wolfe called "the right stuff" — knows and understands these risks, and accepts them without comment. They often say things to friends and family like, "If I have to die, I hope it's doing what I love the most — sailing through the heavens, being an astronaut."

As the crew of STS-107 completed their final chores, Columbia flew over the Earth at an altitude of more than 200 miles at approximately 20 times the speed of sound. Occasionally, the astronauts took a moment to gaze out of a window at the brilliant blues and browns and greens of the planet below them. Kalpana Chawla, who was on her second shuttle mission and had logged an impressive total of 6.5 million miles in space, commented about the majestic Himalayan Mountains that grace her native India. It was an awe-inspiring sight, and one of the last images of Earth that Chawla saw before she died.

At approximately 7 a.m. Eastern Standard Time the astronauts finished the last systems checks in the crew module and confirmed that the ship was in the correct position for re-entry. Their final destination was Cape Canaveral, Florida which, at that particular moment, was still blanketed in light morning fog. Visibility was poor, but NASA officials were confident that the mist would burn away well before Columbia's arrival two hours later. In fact, agency meteorologists were predicting a gorgeous day, just as it had been when Columbia lifted off 16 days before.

At 8:15 a.m. EST, over the Indian Ocean at an altitude of 176 miles, Commander Husband and Pilot McCool were given approval by Mission Control for a braking maneuver known as the de-orbit burn. At the time, Columbia was flying upside down and backward. (To the astronauts, however, the position of the craft meant nothing; in the weightlessness of space, there is no up or down.) Given the go ahead, several rockets were fired to slow the speeding craft in preparation for descent, a process that took two minutes and 38 seconds. The shuttle's computers then slowly moved the craft around into a nose-up position for re-entry.

Flying a shuttle during re-entry and landing is usually uneventful, but it's far from easy. In fact, many astronauts compare it to flying a brick with wings. Computers guide the ship during much of re-entry, and the pilot takes control only after the shuttle emerges from what's known as the plasma stage. Maintaining control during this part of the return, even with the assistance of computers, is tricky because the shuttle is essentially a huge glider that requires sweeping S-turns to slow it down. The pilot and commander must constantly monitor dozens of dials and indicators measuring deceleration, temperature, hydraulics and other factors to make sure the craft is on course, flying smoothly and approaching the landing area at just the right angle.

At around 8:45 a.m. EST, Columbia began entry interface and penetrated the outer fringes of Earth's atmosphere a little north of Hawaii at an altitude of 400,000 feet, a pink glow surrounding the craft as atmospheric friction heated her 30,000-plus protective tiles. As the shuttle continued its rapid descent, the glow went from pink to red to searing white. The special tiles get so hot — almost 3,000 degrees F. in some places — that what's known as a plasma shield (a buffer of heated gases) surrounds the ship, making communication with Mission Control impossible for a brief period.

So far, everything had gone extremely smoothly. Mission Control in Houston was pleased with Columbia's mission, and there was no reason to anticipate that its return home would be anything but problem-free. At Cape Canaveral, the weather had cleared up just as NASA meteorologists had predicted, with the temperature in the low 70s and a light breeze at the landing strip. As the minutes ticked down to the shuttle's triumphant return, the viewing stands filled with the astronauts' excited families and friends, NASA officials and various bigwigs, many of whom had never witnessed a shuttle landing up close before. Members of the shuttle pit crew were standing by to take possession of the ship and transport it back to its hangar just as soon as the astronauts disembarked and the cheering crowds dispersed.

In Houston, the highly trained members of Mission Control watched their monitors and chatted among themselves, confident that the most difficult aspect of their job was nearly done. Their biggest concern that day had been the weather, but their worries had been baseless with ideal weather at Cape Canaveral and nearly every other contingency landing strip around the world. A few minutes more and they could log another successful mission and begin preparing for the next one.

The ease at Mission Control was not to last. At 8:53 a.m. EST, as Columbia sailed over San Francisco, a data point on various monitors began to flicker, indicating a halt in the flow of information regarding the temperature of the hydraulic systems in the ship's left wing. This by itself was not a point of concern because systems monitors routinely glitched; in fact, Mission

Control didn't even notify the crew. But just three minutes later, as the ship cruised over Utah, the temperature in the left landing gear and brake lining suddenly spiked by nearly 60 degrees. Two minutes after that, three temperature sensors buried in the skin on Columbia's left flank went dead.

Columbia was at an altitude of approximately 40 miles and flying at more than 18 times the speed of sound, or around 13,200 miles per hour. It was still 1,400 miles from its destination, a trip that would have taken another 16 minutes. At that moment, the shuttle was in a left-bank, with its wings angled at about 57 degrees to the horizontal. It was also experiencing increasing drag on its left side, something the ship's automatic flight control systems were struggling to correct.

Mission controllers battled to make sense of the faltering systems. What the hell was going on? One sensor going dead was probably no big deal, but several in a matter of minutes combined with the temperature spike suggested trouble. Big trouble. Moments later, as Columbia flew over Texas at an altitude of 207,000 feet, Spacecraft Communicator Charlie Hobaugh radioed the crew.

"Columbia, Houston," he said, "we see your tire-pressure message."

"Roger," Commander Husband replied. "Buh . . ."

Commander Husband's comment was cut off as voice communications suddenly went dead. It was as if someone had literally pulled the plug. Communication with the ship's hundreds of systems — a constant stream of technical information known as telemetry — also ceased. By then Houston knew that something had gone terribly wrong.

Hobaugh tried to regain contact. "Columbia, Houston," he said. "Com check." Nothing but static. "Columbia, Houston. UHF com check." Mission controllers switched channels, hoping desperately to hear Commander Husband's voice. But again they heard only static.

"Columbia, Houston," Hobaugh called several more times. No response. Dread set in as the reality of the situation became apparent. In the moments that followed, the newer members of Mission Control remained hopeful that communication could somehow be restored, that the problem was only a minor technical glitch; the veterans on the crew knew otherwise. The sudden loss of crew and ship communication and the spike in temperature on the ship's left side could mean only one thing: Columbia was gone. "We lost all vehicle data," Chief Flight Director Milt Heflin said later. "That's when we began to know that we had a bad day."

Meanwhile, family members of the seven Columbia astronauts were gathered at the

Kennedy Space Center in Florida, eyes glued to the skies, ready to welcome their loved ones back to earth. As the scheduled landing time approached, the families even began a countdown from 10 to zero, waiting for the shuttle to appear. Then everyone fell silent as they realized the shuttle would not be landing.

"Just like at the liftoff, we counted back from 10, but we got to zero and nothing," said Rona Ramon, Israeli astronaut Ilan's wife. "No sign — the shuttle wasn't drawing near, nor did we hear the sonic booms that we knew would be heard before the landing. There was an odd, terrible quiet. As the minutes passed, we already knew there was nobody to wait for."

Choking back tears, Rona said she and her four children had received e-mails from Ilan during the space flight — the last coming just moments before the shuttle prepared for landing. After the tragedy, Ramon's 5-year-old daugher Noa asked her mother, "How can you die in space? People are supposed to die only on Earth."

Ramon's father, Elizer Wolferman, was in the midst of a live TV interview in Jerusalem, recalling the last time he'd spoken to his hero son, when news of the disaster reached Israel. The interviewer cut him off. A few hours later, the devastated father went before the cameras again, his pride turned to unspeakable anguish.

"I think of everything from the day he was born until now," he said. "I have no son. It is very sad, and I don't know what else to say."

After NASA lost contact with the shuttle, family members were ushered into crew quarters and given the grim news. They were kept in seclusion.

Two days after the catastrophe, Evelyn Husband, wife of astronaut Rick Husband, read a statement from the families:

"On January 16 we saw our loved ones launch into a brilliant, cloud-free sky. Their hearts were full of enthusiasm, pride in country, faith in their God and a willingness to accept risk in the pursuit of knowledge — knowledge that might improve the quality of life for all mankind.

"Although we grieve deeply, as do the families of Apollo 1 and Challenger before us, the bold exploration of space must go on."

Audrey McCool, mother of astronaut William McCool, reinforced that sentiment: "We want the space mission to go on. We don't want those people to have died in vain. The worst is when I have to look at his picture on the television. It was such a perfect mission. It was so perfect."

Astronaut Laurel Clark's brother, Daniel Salton, who'd risen at 5 a.m. to monitor the shuttle's return, agreed: "It had been an absolutely flawless flight. To have this happen with 15 minutes to go until it was over was just unbelievable. I'm just glad she got to get up to space and got to see it because that had been a dream for a long time."

For Clark's aunt and uncle, Betty and Doug Haviland of Ames, Iowa, the shuttle accident brought back horrific memories of another tragedy — their son Timothy died in the World Trade Center collapse.

At around 8 a.m. CST, just minutes before the astronauts' families learned that Columbia had been lost, a series of deafening explosions rocked the Texas plains from high above. In Nacogdoches County and surrounding areas, people jolted awake or raced to windows to see what had happened. The explosions were so loud that many said they initially believed that a train had derailed or a plane had crashed. Some sent up silent prayers, just to be safe.

Moments before the explosions, excited space buffs had been scanning the clear skies for the first glimpse of Columbia as it arced overhead on its way home. Instead, and without warning, they heard the booms and saw the long, white contrails as flaming pieces of the doomed shuttle separated from the main craft like shooting stars. A huge white plume of smoke confirmed the worst, and many observers immediately thought back to January 28, 1986, when similar plumes accompanied the destruction of Challenger.

As he filmed the shuttle's re-entry as a favor to CNN, John Pronk, a cameraman with WFAA-TV in Dallas, captured Columbia's final moments as it plummeted earthward. James Lenamon, a cameraman for KXAS-TV in Dallas, also shot footage of the shuttle breaking apart, but as he filed the footage he had no idea that anything had gone wrong, and went on to his next assignment — to videotape parents waiting in line at a private school.

Because of the break in radio contact with Columbia, no one knows for sure if the astronauts were aware of their fate in the ship's final seconds or if they were alive when it disintegrated. The shuttle's cockpit is a sturdy structure, but certainly not strong enough to survive the structural instability that tore Columbia apart. Still, there could have been a few seconds in which they knew the end had come. It certainly had to have been a faster, less traumatic death than the one that met the crew of Challenger. Analysis of that disaster revealed that those astronauts were probably alive during the tortuous two-minute, 45-second plunge into the Atlantic Ocean.

Moments after Columbia's destruction, hell rained on Texas in the form of thousands of pieces of flaming debris. In downtown Nacogdoches, hundreds of smoldering chunks of twisted metal bombarded streets, yards and buildings. One piece crashed through the roof of an optometrist's office and landed on a desk, where it stayed until investigators arrived to claim it. According to witnesses, many pieces of debris were burned so badly that they looked like charcoal. In San Augustine, Texas, people recoiled in horror as they stumbled across charred body parts.

Because of Columbia's speed and trajectory, the main debris area initially stretched from Palestine, Texas into Louisiana and Arkansas, a swath totaling more than 500 square miles. Pieces of the shuttle struck homes, businesses, schools and other structures, but miraculously no one on the ground — with the exception of a dog which was reportedly struck and killed by falling debris — was injured. However, there appeared to be some close calls. According to one unconfirmed rumor, a chunk of debris plunged through a roof and struck an unoccupied dentist's chair.

Several large pieces of debris, some said to be the size of a compact car, plunged into the Toledo Bend Reservoir near the Texas-Louisiana border. "I heard the piece coming down through the air," said Elbie Bradley, who was fishing there at the time. "It sounded like it was fluttering." NASA investigators later used sonar to locate the pieces and mark their location for future retrieval.

Jim Stutzman of Nacogdoches found a nine-inch-long, two-inch-wide piece of metal in his yard. "It had heat burns, melted metal and some of the grass burned into it when it fell," he said.

In a bid to keep a curious public at bay, NASA immediately issued a warning that no debris should be touched, due to the tremendous risk posed by the shuttle's highly volatile liquid propellant and other potential hazards. Nonetheless, many residents simply picked up the debris they found in their yards and brought it to authorities.

Four extremely toxic compounds are used as fuel or coolant aboard every shuttle — raw hydrazine, monomethyl hydrazine, nitrogen tetroxide and pure ammonia. All can result in very serious health problems if absorbed or inhaled, which is why NASA officials were so concerned at the thought of unknowing civilians picking up and pocketing materials they found on the ground. Other potential hazards included the silica fibers used in the heat-resistant tiles, which can cause serious lung damage if inhaled, and the unlikely — but still possible — existence of pyrotechnical devices, such as the explosive bolts used to blow the shuttle hatch in an emergency.

Local law enforcement and National Guard reservists were immediately enlisted to locate fallen debris and protect it until it could be collected by NASA, the Environmental Protection Agency or Air Force ordnance disposal experts. Guard duty wasn't an easy task because of the size of the debris field and the tremendous number of pieces to be recovered. In Nacogdoches County alone, more than 2,000 pieces were reported. In many cases, much of the original debris field was relatively untouched forest and field, which made recovery tedious and difficult. Rainy weather also hampered recovery efforts and forced searchers to use all-terrain vehicles and horses. Later, manned motorized parachutes capable of skimming treetops at just 200 feet above the ground were also enlisted in the search.

Although very few pieces of the shuttle were recovered outside the initial swath, in the days following the disaster the debris field was found to extend west into Arizona and California. As word spread, so did false reports — hundreds of them. Anything unusual found in someone's back yard was immediately believed to be a piece of Columbia, including a truck's mud flap, a discarded automobile alternator and even a piece of burnt toast. But officials dutifully came by to pick up whatever was reported, no matter how unlikely, because they simply couldn't take the chance that it really was a part of the doomed shuttle.

Less than a week after Columbia's demise, more than 12,000 pieces of debris had been collected. Of that number, several hundred had been verified as authentic shuttle parts. Some were as small as a matchbook while others were so large they had to be transported by truck. One of the larger pieces — the shuttle's nosecone — was recovered in a forest south of Hemphill, Texas. It showed little damage from the intense heat of re-entry. In a field near Lufkin, Texas, searchers found a helmet thought to belong to one of the shuttle's crew members.

Investigators later announced the recovery of several other important pieces of debris, including a harness, a shoe, strips of clothing and a 700-pound rocket engine that had punched a 12-foot hole in the ground and thrown dirt 35 feet into the air.

Meanwhile, search crews near the east Texas town of Bronson hunted for a top-secret object believed to be a communications device that handled encrypted messages between the shuttle and Mission Control. Investigators kept mum, but various press reports speculated that the device was in a government "telecommunications security" category that required extremely tight precautions. Searchers, who had been given only a picture of a faceplate from the device, which said "Secret Government Property," meticulously combed through dense underbrush in the hope that the mysterious cargo had survived the explosion that tore the shuttle apart. The press was kept at a distance by Texas state troopers, who told the newsmen that they would be required to leave if searchers found something that could not be photographed. In the end, however, nothing of significance was recovered.

Because of the rough, wooded terrain that covers much of the debris field, it's likely that parts of Columbia will be discovered by hunters, campers and hikers for years to come. "In many areas, it's impossible to search," James Kroll, director of the Forestry Resources Institute at Stephen F. Austin State University, told a reporter. "It's my prediction that 10 years from now, there'll be hunters in the woods that find pieces, maybe big pieces."

As with other tragedies before it, the Columbia disaster brought out both the best and the worst in mankind. Most Americans felt saddened by the accident and offered heartfelt prayers and tributes to the fallen astronauts. However, some immediately recognized the event as an opportunity to make a quick buck. Within hours of the shuttle's destruction, online auction sites such as eBay were inundated with "rare" Columbia or other shuttle memorabilia. A Columbia pencil sharpener sold for $6, astronaut salt and pepper shakers drew high bids of $15 and one motivated seller was offering a brass urn with a picture of Columbia for $200.

Even mission patches, which sell for less than $5 at the Smithsonian Institute in Washington,

D.C., the Kennedy Space Center in Florida and The Space Store in Houston, were being listed as rare collectibles and demanding upwards of $100. In truth, the patches are extremely common, said officials at A-B Emblem, the Weaverville, North Carolina company that has manufactured mission patches for NASA since Apollo 11 in 1969. Nearly 30,000 patches for STS-107 were produced prior to lift-off, and the company quickly began producing more to meet demand in the days following the tragedy. Interestingly, several mission patches were found among Columbia's debris. It's believed that the recovered patches accompanied the astronauts into orbit as souvenirs.

Most disturbing of all was the auction of an item titled "Columbia Space Shuttle Debris," which had an opening bid of $10,000. It was quickly removed by eBay officials.

NASA had to deal with similar problems following the destruction of Challenger 17 years before. Because that shuttle exploded over the Atlantic ocean, recovery was difficult and debris continued to wash ashore for months and even years afterward. Realizing the collector value of anything related to Challenger, many unscrupulous individuals tried to sell bogus items to the gullible. In one case, a California man framed a common bathroom tile, added a plaque and tried to sell it for several hundred dollars as a genuine piece of the doomed ship. NASA security intervened before he could pull off the scam.

Sometimes, however, the real thing pops up. In 1989, the NASA Security Office received a call from a Florida shop owner who had been approached by a man looking to sell an official Challenger mission patch for $20,000. Investigators assumed the patch was phony — a souvenir available for a couple of bucks at the Kennedy Space Center. But it turned out to be authentic, one of 25 patches carried aboard the shuttle as mementos. Investigators were tipped off by the patch's manufacturing insignia and its bleached appearance, suggesting it had been under water for a long time. The box containing the patches had apparently been dredged up by a fishing boat.

Just four days after Columbia went down, federal agents in east Texas made their first arrests for shuttle debris theft. A student was charged with removing clumps of thermal coating from a soccer field, while another individual was charged with stealing a circuit board while posing as a NASA official. Both faced ten years in prison and a $250,000 fine.

At the same time, U.S. attorneys in Texas announced a two-day grace period for people to turn in shuttle debris without facing prosecution. "That thing you may be holding in your pocket, on your desk or on your mantle could be the single piece that saves the lives of future astronauts," said Michael T. Shelby, U.S. attorney for the Southern District of Texas. "This isn't about prosecuting people. It's about trying to gather as much debris as we can to figure out what happened."

Still, some people couldn't help but hang on to their morbid souvenirs. On February 10, a man was charged with theft of government property for allegedly stealing a piece of tile and other small shuttle debris while helping a state task force in the search effort. He was released on a $5,000 bond.

Within days, NASA — working with the Federal Emergency Management Agency — set up a system to help residents and businesses file claims to pay for damage resulting from the falling shuttle debris. Those wishing to file claims had two years to do so, and were instructed to call the Emergency Operations Center at Johnson Space Center. Participants were eligible for either cash or low-interest loans.

Far more gruesome than collecting debris was the task of recovering and identifying the remains of Columbia's crew. In Hemphill, Texas, two boys, ages 6 and 4, came across a charred human leg while taking a ride across a field on their dad's four-wheeler. A woman's arm, a mutilated torso, a thigh bone and skull were also recovered from various rural locations within hours of the shuttle's destruction and taken to Dover Air Force Base in Delaware, where military pathologists performed DNA and other testing to ensure positive identification. The remains of Ilan Ramon were the first to be identified, using dental records that matched a jaw found on the ground.

The White House first learned that Columbia was lost when chief of staff Andrew Card saw preliminary reports while channel — flipping in his cabin at Camp David. His first thought was that the shuttle had somehow been brought down by terrorists — understandable considering that an Israeli war hero was one of its crew members — so he immediately called the White House Situation Room. He then notified President George W. Bush, who was in his cabin preparing for his morning workout. Shocked by the news, the president arranged to return directly to Washington by motorcade and scheduled a 12:45 p.m. conference call with the families of the lost astronauts.

Fifteen minutes before the call, President Bush reviewed the crew members' biographies and found out which of them had spouses and families. It was obvious that the disaster had hit the president very hard. On the phone with the astronauts' shocked and grief-stricken families, still gathered in NASA crew quarters, he told them, "I wish I was there to hug and to cry and to comfort you.

"Tough day, tough day," he murmured as he left the Oval Office to compose himself for the delivery of the sad news to the nation. His eyes glistening with tears, the president said:

My fellow Americans, this day has brought terrible news and great sadness to our country. At 9:00 this morning, Mission Control in Houston lost contact with our space shuttle Columbia. A short time later, debris was seen falling from the skies above Texas. The Columbia is lost. There were no survivors.

On board was a crew of seven — Colonel Rick Husband, Lieutenant Colonel Michael Anderson, Commander Laurel Clark, Captain David Brown, Commander William McCool, Dr. Kalpana Chawla, and Ilan Ramon, a colonel in the Israeli air force.

These men and women assumed great risk in this service to all humanity. In an age when space flight has come to seem almost routine, it is easy to overlook the dangers of travel by rocket and the difficulties of navigating the fierce outer atmosphere of the earth.

These astronauts knew the dangers, and they faced them willingly, knowing they had a high and noble purpose in life. Because of their courage and daring and idealism, we will miss them all the more.

All Americans today are thinking, as well, of the families of these men and women who have been given this sudden shock and grief. You're not alone. Our entire nation grieves with you. And those you loved will always have the respect and gratitude of this country.

The cause in which they died will continue. Mankind is led into the darkness beyond our world by the inspiration of discovery and the longing to understand. Our journey into space will go on.

In the skies today, we saw destruction and tragedy. Yet farther than we can see, there is comfort and hope. In the words of the prophet Isaiah, 'Lift your eyes and look to the heavens. Who created all these? He who brings out the starry hosts one by one and calls them each by name. Because of His great power and mighty strength, not one of them is missing.'

The same creator who names the stars also knows the names of the seven souls we mourn today. The crew of the shuttle Columbia did not return safely to Earth, yet we can pray that all are safely home.

May God bless the grieving families, and may God continue to bless America.

President Bush's comments reflected the

tattered emotions of the American people as they sat glued to their televisions. Coming so soon after the terrorist attacks of September 11, 2001, it was another national tragedy that many found difficult to bear.

* * *

News of the shuttle disaster broke within moments of its occurrence, and the major networks immediately began continuous coverage, airing over and over the agonizing footage of Columbia's fatal plunge, updating the news as it came in and speculating when they had nothing new. All manner of experts were paraded before the cameras to give their thoughts on what might have gone wrong.

In the rush to stay on top of the story, many mistakes were made and inaccuracies reported. CNN briefly ran a scroll noting that the shuttle had been flying at 18 times the speed of light, instead of the more accurate 18 times the speed of sound. A television correspondent accidentally called former astronaut Buzz Aldrin "Buzz Armstrong," confusing his name with Neil Armstrong who, accompanied by Aldrin aboard Apollo 11, became the first man to set foot on the surface of the moon.

NASA officials did their best to provide information to the demanding members of the press, but in the first hours of the disaster there was little to give. Theories were mentioned but the fact was, they really didn't know what had happened.

Worse, these weren't faceless individuals NASA officials were being asked to discuss, they were, in many cases, men and women with whom they had worked very closely for many years. And now they were gone — suddenly, violently and very, very publicly. Many tears were shed in front of the unblinking eye of the television camera, and many more were shed behind closed doors.

Across the world people from every nation tried to come to grips with what had happened. Over the years, a total of 30 nations have sent astronauts into space as part of the space shuttle program, so the loss of Columbia truly was an international tragedy. Almost immediately, international condolences poured out: In a brief a telephone call to Israeli Prime Minister Ariel Sharon, Russian President Vladimir Putin expressed his sincerest condolences regarding the loss of Israel's first astronaut, Ilan Ramon, whom President Putin described as an excellent man and a person of hope. He added that Ramon's death was a painful loss for the Israeli people.

Grief was especially profound among the people of India, millions of whom had closely followed the progress of the Columbia mission and crew member Kalpana Chawla who, though a naturalized U.S. citizen, was considered a hero by many in her native country. "For us in India, the fact that one of them was an India-born woman adds a special poignancy to the tragedy," Prime Minister Atal Behari Vajpayee wrote to President Bush. "We convey our heartfelt sympathies at the tragedy which has overtaken space shuttle Columbia. We mourn with you in this moment of grief."

The European Space Agency (ESA) issued a statement from its Paris headquarters calling the shuttle's loss "a devastating event in the history of space." ESA officials added, "The ESA shares in the grief that struck NASA and the whole space community today."

The one nation that did not send condolences was Iraq, who seemed just weeks away from war with the United States when Columbia went down. Iraqi President Saddam Hussein said the tragedy was God's way of punishing the United States for its aggressive actions.

As the world reeled following the Columbia tragedy, impromptu memorials to the fallen astronauts began appearing all across a grief-stricken America. At Cape Canaveral, more than 500 people gathered to share a moment of silence around the Astronaut Memorial, a 51-foot-high black granite wall bearing the names of astronauts who have died in the line of duty. New wreaths were laid at the base of the memorial beside those left to commemorate the 17th anniversary of the Challenger explosion on January 28.

"We've all hoped and prayed many times that no names would be added to this wall," said Stephen Feldman, president of the Astronaut Memorial Foundation.

The white fence in front of the memorial was adorned with roses, daisies, lilacs and tulips. "May all your dreams continue," read a card on one bouquet. Another note said: "Our tears are not only those of sorrow but also tears of pride. You will never be forgotten."

In Houston, flowers piled up outside the gates of the Johnson Space Center, which quickly became a shrine to the lost astronauts. Many mourners lit candles, knelt, and prayed together. Dozens of hand-written signs accompanied photos of the astronauts. One sign read: "All the precious lives lost today on board Columbia — we mourn you."

Not far away in Nacogdoches, flowers were laid by taped-off areas around a piece of metal that fell from the sky. At the Goddard Space Flight Center in Greenbelt, Maryland — where American and Israeli scientists worked before the Columbia mission — flags were at half-staff.

Visitors to the Smithsonian's National Air and

Space Museum in Washington, D.C., left flowers and candles in memoriam to the Columbia astronauts. One hand-written note praised the crew for making "the ultimate sacrifice in the pursuit of knowledge." Many visitors came to have their photo taken beside a 12-foot-tall model of Columbia and to sign a condolence book. The day after the disaster, visitor Frank Lanky said: "Yesterday reminded everyone how out of our hands it all is."

In Hawaii, workers at the Onizuka Space Center set up a memorial with flowers and a photo of the Columbia crew. Visitors included Claude Onizuka, whose brother Ellison died in the Challenger explosion. "It reopened the wound," he said.

At the National Hockey League All-Star Game in Sunrise, Florida — and other sports venues across the nation — players and spectators observed a moment of silence in memory of the Columbia astronauts.

In Afghanistan, somber American troops gathered at a standing-room-only service at Bagram Air Base and said prayers for the shuttle crew. Soldiers sang hymns after tucking their weapons under their seats.

In Clear Lake City, Texas, mourners packed Grace Community Church and fought back tears as they watched images of astronauts Rick Husband and Michael Anderson, who were regular congregants, as they talked about their love of flying and asked for prayers.

The disaster even hit the entertainment industry. Paramount Pictures immediately asked theaters to pull a preview trailer for the movie The Core, which contained a scene in which a disabled space shuttle is forced to make an emergency landing in Los Angeles. However, the studio said it had no plans to pull the scene from the film or change its March 28 release date.

Hewlett-Packard asked magazines to pull a print ad the company had recently introduced featuring astronauts and NASA. In all but a few instances, the requests were made in time for the ad to be withdrawn before further publication. A company spokesperson said the ad would be replaced with another in the same campaign, which carried the theme "Everything is Possible."

A few days after the disaster President George Bush presided over a memorial service at Johnson Space Center, offering personal remembrances of each of the seven astronauts. Here's the text of his speech:

Their mission was almost complete and we lost them so close to home. The men and women of the Columbia had journeyed more than six million miles and were minutes away from arrival and reunion. The loss was sudden and terrible, and for their families the grief is heavy. Our nation joins in your sorrow and in your pride.

We remember not only one moment of tragedy, but seven lives of great purpose and achievement. To leave behind Earth and air and gravity is an ancient dream of humanity. For these seven it was a dream fulfilled. Each of these astronauts had the daring and discipline required of their calling. Each of them knew that great endeavors are inseparable from great risks. And each of them accepted those risks willingly, even joyfully, in the cause of discovery.

Rick Husband was a boy of four when he first thought of being an astronaut. As a man and having become an astronaut, he found it was even more important to love his family and serve his Lord. One of Rick's favorite hymns was How Great Thou Art, which offers these words of praise: 'I see the stars. I hear the mighty thunder. Thy power throughout the universe displayed.'

David Brown was first drawn to the stars as a little boy with a telescope in his backyard. He admired astronauts, but as he said: 'I thought they were movie stars. I thought I was kind of a normal kid.' David grew up to be a physician, an aviator who could land on the deck of a carrier in the middle of the night, and a shuttle astronaut. His brother asked him several weeks ago, what would happen if something went wrong on their mission.

David replied, 'This program will go on.'

Michael Anderson always wanted to fly planes and rose to the rank of lieutenant colonel in the Air Force. Along the way, he became a role model, especially for his two daughters and for the many children he spoke to in schools. He said to them, 'Whatever you want to be in life, you're training for it now.' He also told his minister, 'If this thing doesn't come out right, don't worry about me, I'm just going on higher.'

Laurel Salton Clark was a physician and a flight surgeon who loved adventure, loved her work, loved her husband and her son. A friend who heard Laurel speaking to Mission Control said, 'There was a smile in her voice.' Laurel conducted some of the experiments as Columbia orbited the Earth and described seeing new life emerge from a tiny cocoon. 'Life,' she said, 'continues in a lot of places, and life is a magical thing.'

None of our astronauts traveled a longer path to space than Kalpana Chawla. She left India as a student, but she would see the nation of her birth, all of it, from hundreds of miles above. When the sad news reached her hometown, an administrator at her high school recalled, 'She always said she wanted to reach the stars.' She went there and beyond. Kalpana's native country mourns her today and so does her adopted land.

Ilan Ramon also flew above his home, the land

of Israel. He said, 'The quiet that envelops space makes the beauty even more powerful, and I only hope that the quiet can one day spread to my country.' Ilan was a patriot, the devoted son of a Holocaust survivor, who served his country in two wars. 'Ilan,' said his wife Rona, 'left us at his peak moment, in his favorite place, with people he loved.'

The Columbia's pilot was Commander Willy McCool, whom friends knew as the most steady and dependable of men. In Lubbock today, they're thinking back to the Eagle Scout who became a distinguished naval officer and a fearless test pilot. One friend remembers Willy this way, 'He was blessed, and we were blessed to know him.'

Our whole nation was blessed to have such men and women serving in our space program. Their loss is deeply felt, especially in this place where so many of you called them friends, the people of NASA are being tested once again. In your grief, you are responding as your friends would have wished, with focus, professionalism and unbroken faith in the mission of this agency.

. . .They go in peace for all mankind, and all mankind is in their debt. Yet, some explorers do not return, and the law settles unfairly on a few. The families here today shared in the courage of those they loved, but now they must face life and grief without them. The sorrow is lonely, but you are not alone. In time, you will find comfort and the grace to see you through. And in God's own time, we can pray that the day of your reunion will come.

And to the children who miss your mom or dad so much today, you need to know they love you, and that love will always be with you. They were proud of you, and you can be proud of them for the rest of your life.

The final days of their own lives were spent looking down upon this earth, and now, on every continent, in every land they can see, the names of these astronauts are known and remembered. They will always have an honored place in the memory of this country and today I offer the respect and gratitude of the people of the United States. May God bless you all.

* * *

Other United States government leaders honored the crew of Columbia in Washington National Cathedral on Thursday, February 6, calling them ambassadors to the universe who met their deaths while trying to improve life on Earth. "They were bound together in the great cause of discovery. They were envoys to the unknown," said Vice President Dick Cheney. "They advanced human understanding by showing human courage."

During the memorial, which was attended by mourners wearing space shuttle lapel pins, singer Patti LaBelle performed Way Up There, a song about the wonder of space travel. Many mourners broke into tears during the song, reminded that their friends and loved ones died doing what they had always dreamed of doing — exploring the great unknown.

Meeting later with friends and family members of the fallen astronauts, NASA Administrator Sean O'Keefe pledged that the agency would find the cause of the accident and proceed with its mission of science and space exploration. "We will persevere," O'Keefe promised. "We will not let you down."

Chapter 2
The Search for Answers

NASA officials began the arduous task of determining what went wrong with Columbia within minutes of the shuttle's destruction. The doors to Mission Control were locked; no one could go in or out, nor were they allowed to make outgoing phone calls. Though overcome with grief, they knew that their only hope of keeping the 30-year-old shuttle program on track was finding the cause of the disaster quickly enough to ensure that it would never happen again. So for the next several hours, mission controllers stored the data in their computers, finished reports and wrote very detailed personal accounts of what they saw, heard and did that fateful morning.

The accidental loss of a shuttle and crew had far-reaching consequences, as NASA learned following the destruction of Challenger 17 years earlier. NASA administrators knew that hardcore space buffs would continue to support the agency and its various scientific programs, but they also knew that many members of Congress, which controls NASA's budget, and an even greater number of ordinary citizens would again scream for an investigation into the cost-versus-benefits of the shuttle program and strongly question its need.

Just as anticipated, vocal anti-shuttle voices were out in force within hours of Columbia's demise. And they had a lot of ammunition. Well before Columbia's tragic date with disaster, NASA's shuttle fleet had been riddled with safety problems:

In August 1994, astronauts aboard Endeavor endured a terrifying last-second launch abort because of an overheated pump in one of the engines. The countdown clock had actually reached zero.

A hydrogen leak delayed Columbia's launch in July 1999.

Discovery was grounded with damaged wiring, a contaminated engine and a dented fuel line in December 1999.

A month later, Endeavor's mission was held up because of bad wiring and computer failures.

Atlantis's main engine had to be replaced in March 2000 because of defective engine seals. Amazingly, these parts had been trashed, but somehow found their way back onto the manned craft.

In August 2000, an inspection of Columbia revealed 3,500 defects in the wiring.

A misplaced safety pin and concerns with the external tank postponed the milestone 100th shuttle flight.

A hydrogen leak forced a scrub of the Atlantis flight in April 2002.

All this, of course, was old news. In the days following the Columbia tragedy, NASA officials had more important things to deal with. Foremost was the thought that the entire shuttle fleet might have to be grounded for the months or years that an investigation could take, as had happened following the Challenger disaster. The idea was distressing because the space shuttle played an integral role in the construction and maintenance of the International Space Station (ISS).

At the time of Columbia's destruction, the station was home to two Americans and a Russian, all of whom were scheduled to be replaced by a fresh crew in March. Keeping the men aboard was not a problem, NASA officials noted, because the station routinely received restocking visits from an unmanned Russian supply vehicle. However, there were bigger concerns, particularly in regard to the ISS's ongoing construction — a task that relied almost exclusively on American space shuttles because of their ability to carry large, heavy components. The unspoken message was clear: The United States is vital to the success of the space station program because Russia can't handle it alone, so our shuttles have to keep flying.

Answers were needed, and quickly.

While search crews in several states struggled to recover as much debris from the fallen shuttle as they could find, NASA investigators tried to determine exactly what might have brought down the mighty steel bird. NASA Administrator Sean O'Keefe said that two investigating boards would be established, one within the space agency and an outside board, headed by retired Admiral Harold W. Gehman Jr., that would take an independent look at the accident. Joining Gehman on the commission was:

✴ Rear Adm. Stephen Turcotte, Commander of the U.S. Naval Safety Center in Norfolk, Virginia.

✴ Maj. Gen. John L. Barry, Director of Plans and Programs for Headquarters Air Force Materiel Command at Wright-Patterson Air Force Base in Ohio.

✴ Maj. Gen. Kenneth W. Hess, Commander and Air Force Chief of Safety at Kirtland Air Force Base in New Mexico.

∗ James N. Hallock, Chief of the Aviation Safety Division for the Transportation Department.

∗ Steven B. Wallace, Director of the Federal Aviation Administration's office of Accident Investigation.

∗ Brig. Gen. Duane Deal, Commander of the 21st Space Wing at Peterson Air Force Base in Colorado.

The House Science Committee, Chaired by Rep. Sherwood Boehlert of New York, also announced its own investigation. "The NASA investigation will focus more on the technical aspects," Boehlert said during a television interview. "We have to be concerned about the policy aspects and what is the future of human space flight."

At the time of the commission announcements, NASA had already requested help from the National Transportation Safety Board (NTSB), which quickly sent a team of six investigators to Barksdale Air Force Base in Bossier City, Louisiana, near the Texas border. Assistance was also requested of the Federal Aviation Administration (FAA), the U.S. Army and the U.S. Navy.

The NTSB, which investigates all disasters involving planes and trains, didn't waste any time. Shortly after being contacted by NASA, the Board requested radar and voice communications data from the FAA's air traffic control facilities in Texas. The radar captures aircraft, which usually fly no higher than 50,000 feet, but would also have picked up images of the shuttle debris that fell following Columbia's disintegration.

Investigators also hoped to recover the so-called "black boxes" that recorded Columbia's flight data. However, because the boxes are not hardened like those on airplanes, NASA officials said it was unlikely the devices survived the crash. It wasn't a devastating loss, though. According to NASA engineers, the boxes usually aren't as critical to a shuttle investigation as they are to a plane investigation because of a process known as telemetry, in which tremendous amounts of flight data are transmitted in real time to Mission Control in Houston.

Due to its importance, all flight data recorded since Columbia's launch on January 16 was immediately impounded, including hundreds of readings on everything from the position of flight control surfaces to tire pressure, a wealth of information that investigators hoped might shed important light on exactly what went wrong.

As investigators geared up for the long haul, the private companies that construct, maintain and repair the shuttles in conjunction with

NASA came under scrutiny. Boeing and Lockheed Martin, under a joint partnership known as the United Space Alliance, are the prime contractors to NASA on the space shuttle program. The United Space Alliance was awarded a $9 billion contract to operate the program between 1996 and 2002, and received an additional $2.9 billion to continue the contract through September 2004. The alliance subcontracts much of the work to smaller companies, with Boeing being the primary subcontractor.

Boeing was instrumental in a major refurbishing of Columbia in 2000 and 2001, and NASA inspectors said from the beginning that they would be taking a close look at the overhaul, which was performed at the Boeing plant in Palmdale, California. At that point, no wrong-doing was suspected on the part of Boeing, but NASA officials stressed that every aspect of Columbia's maintenance — including the work of smaller subcontractors — would have to be examined as part of the agency's ongoing investigation.

While theories regarding the accident were plentiful, ruled out from the beginning was terrorism. It was, however, an understandable concern given the current state of the world. After all, al-Qaeda sleeper cells were known to be living in the United States, and what better target for Arab extremists than an American space shuttle carrying Israel's first astronaut?

People wondered: Was the ship shot down by some sort of missile? Had a terrorist working within NASA somehow slipped a small bomb aboard? Conspiracy theorists had a field day, but NASA and military officials immediately stepped in to quell public concerns. While a traditional airplane could conceivably be shot down by a ground-to-air missile, Columbia was at far too high an altitude (more than 200,000 feet) and traveling far too fast (Mach 18, or 18 times the speed of sound) for this to be possible. Besides, ground radar didn't pick up anything approaching the ship at the time it disintegrated.

The possibility that a bomb had somehow been planted aboard Columbia prior to liftoff was even less likely, investigators noted. Security at Cape Canaveral, where the shuttles are maintained and launched, had always been tight, and it was tightened even more in the aftermath of the September 11, 2001 terrorist attacks on the Pentagon and the World Trade Center. Visitors touring the facility by bus were no longer allowed near a shuttle on the launch pad, liftoff times were kept secret until 24 hours before launch, the number of security guards was increased and only authorized personnel were allowed anywhere near a shuttle at any time.

Another consideration was the relatively small

confines of Columbia's interior. With seven astronauts living aboard the ship and conducting a wide range of experiments over 16 days, it's safe to assume that virtually every inch of available space was inspected many times, and that anything out of the ordinary would have been spotted and reported immediately.

Not surprisingly, NASA employees were deeply offended at the idea that one of their own might have intentionally tried to destroy Columbia. The men and women who maintain the shuttle fleet and work with the astronauts are an extremely close family, and many of them have been with NASA for decades. That any of them would want to inflict harm was unthinkable.

Rather than terrorism, initial speculation about what caused the accident focused on possible damage to the left wing of the ship during liftoff. An array of videocameras is trained on every part of the shuttle during launch, and at least one of them captured images of what appeared to be a two-foot-long chunk of foam insulation from the 154-foot external fuel tank striking the protective tiles on the left wing as Columbia roared toward the heavens.

The falling insulation was NASA's primary suspect from the start of the investigation, though Shuttle Program Manager Ron Dittemore and others went out of their way to say that it was just one of many theories being considered. "There are a lot of things in this business that look like the smoking gun but turn out not even to be close," Dittemore said.

On February 2, the day after the accident, Dittemore held a press conference during which he noted that technicians had received several signs of an unusual increase in temperatures on Columbia's exterior near the left wheel well shortly before the shuttle went down. In addition, computers detected an increase in drag on the left side, suggesting damage — possibly a missing tile — on the shuttle's protective skin. The findings, Dittemore said, did not conclusively point to the cause of the disaster, but they did provide important pieces to the puzzle.

Dittemore was quick to add that the investigation was less than 30 hours old and that there would likely be many false leads before the root cause was established. "I'm confident that even what I tell you today will be fluid and will change from day to day for a while," Dittemore said, adding that technicians hoped to retrieve 32 additional seconds of data from NASA computers that was believed to have been collected on the ground after Mission Control lost contact with the crew. Those 32 seconds, if they could be found, could very well reveal vital information the investigators so desperately needed.

While the falling foam theory seemed most

likely at the beginning of the investigation, officials were also considering the possible role of an earlier problem — small cracks in the ship's fuel line. In June 2002, cracks were found in the liner of a liquid-hydrogen feed line in the shuttle Atlantis. Similar cracks were found in Endeavor, Discovery and Columbia. As a result, the fleet was grounded for three months so the problem could be repaired, postponing Columbia's original July 2002 launch until January 2003.

Two days after the accident, on February 3, NASA again raised the issue of the piece of foam insulation that struck the leading edge of the shuttle's left wing 80 seconds into launch. "We're making the assumption that the external tank was the root cause of the accident," Dittemore announced. "It is a drastic assumption, and it's sobering, but I think that's what we need to do." In regard to post-launch studies by NASA engineers that concluded the shuttle was not in peril, Dittemore added, "When we wrote the report, I'm not sure we knew what we were talking about."

Dittemore's admission was harrowing in its implications. If correct, it meant that Columbia had been doomed since launch and the crew and those in Mission Control were completely unaware of it throughout the16-day mission.

During that press conference, Dittemore and

others informed reporters that the foam damage had been thoroughly reviewed to the best of NASA's ability with the information available. On January 17, the day after the launch, NASA engineers reviewed the video footage and began their analysis, meeting January 20 to go over their findings. Teams discussed different aspects of risk, with groups ranging in size from 30 to as few as one or two when questions became specialized. By January 22, the engineering analysis had concluded that the risk was not serious, a finding that was confirmed by final reviews on January 23 and 24.

According to Dittemore, NASA officials were briefed on the risk assessment on January 24 and 27. Both meetings confirmed the engineers' conclusion that Columbia was not in jeopardy as a result of the falling insulation.

On January 28, the 12th day of the mission, NASA engineers reported: "The damaged conditions included one tile missing down to (a deep layer) and multiple tiles missing over an area of about 7 inches by 30 inches. These thermal analyses indicate possible localized structural damage but no burn through and no safety of flight issue."

It's important to note that NASA engineers had to make several assumptions during their analysis because the damage was under the shuttle's wing and could not be seen or assessed by the astronauts. Essentially working blind, the engineers started by estimating the size of the object that hit the wing based on the puff of white in video footage that resulted from the insulation disintegrating on impact, and then proceeding from there.

During the February 3 conference, Dittemore also confirmed that the piece of foam in question was determined to be much larger than initially believed — 20 inches long, 16 inches wide, six inches thick and weighing 2.67 pounds. These calculations erred on the side of caution, Dittemore said, suggesting that the chunk of insulation was probably smaller and lighter. From there, the engineers estimated the angle at which the foam struck the wing and concluded that it was probably quite sharp.

Based on these assumptions, NASA engineers tried to deduce the impacts of the foam hitting one tile as well as a larger area. They had no reason to believe that their calculations would be wrong because this technique had worked very well in the past, typically overestimating the amount of damage that had occurred, Dittemore said.

While analysts were uncertain exactly how much damage might have been done to the underside of the left wing, Dittemore estimated that it could have gouged out an area up to 32 inches long, seven inches wide and two inches thick. The engineers' worst-case scenarios were one destroyed tile near the main landing gear door or several partially damaged tiles.

"Even though you might have localized structural damage, you would not have damage sufficient to cause a catastrophic event nor impact the flying qualities of the vehicle," Dittemore said.

In retrospect, had the damage been noticed within the first few minutes of liftoff, the crew of Columbia might have been able to abort the launch and return safely to the Kennedy Space Center. It's a risky and difficult maneuver — and one that's never been performed before — but it would have saved the crew from the perils of re-entry because the shuttle would not yet have reached space. Unfortunately, NASA engineers didn't notice that the chunk of insulation had struck the left wing until they reviewed the launch tapes the next day.

Based on available data at that early stage in the investigation, space agency officials speculated that a series of events, each one triggering the next like falling dominoes, ultimately caused Columbia's fall from the sky. During the final eight minutes of the mission, sensors showed that temperatures on and near the shuttle's left wing rapidly rose to previously unseen levels. According to Dittemore, signs of trouble reported by sensors in the left wheel well most likely were an indication of more serious problems elsewhere.

The question was, where exactly did the primary breach occur? "There's some other event, some other missing link, that is contributing to this event," Dittemore said. "It's a mystery to us, and we seem to have some conflicting information."

The shuttle's wheel wells had been an issue of particular concern as far back as 1990, the New York Times reported on February 5, four days after the accident. The paper noted that a study conducted by researchers at Stanford University and Carnegie Mellon and financed by NASA found the tiles around the wheel wells to be extremely vulnerable to catastrophic failure due to their location near fuel tanks and the shuttle's hydraulics system — some of the craft's most important and volatile sections.

During launch, the tiles are often struck by flying debris and they become spectacularly hot during re-entry. Should they become even moderately damaged over the course of a mission, the shuttle would be placed at incredible risk. In fact, the loss of even one tile could create a "zipper" effect in which adjoining tiles would rip away, exposing the shuttle's outer skin.

(An academic study based on this research and published in 1993 found that tile damage from falling debris had plagued the shuttle program since its early days. In fact, there had been nearly 2,000 significant debris hits in the first 33 shuttle missions.)

The same study also identified the ice that builds up on the ship's extremely cold external fuel tank as a primary source of debris that could fall and damage the shuttle's protective heat tiles, resulting in a chain of events that, under the right circumstances, could doom the ship at liftoff. The day after Columbia went down, NASA headquarters called to request a copy of the study, which the agency had apparently misplaced, said co-author Dr. Elisabeth Pate-Cornell, a researcher at Stamford.

On the same day as the New York Times report, NASA officials reiterated that they still believed the object that struck Columbia during launch was foam insulation, though they added there was growing speculation that it could have been caked with ice. The insulation was bright orange, but the object captured on videotape appeared to be white, or at least light-colored. Based on this assessment, there was growing concern that NASA engineers had grossly underestimated the weight of the object during their initial risk assessment.

During the February 4 news conference, NASA officials confirmed that Columbia had sat on the launch pad for 39 days, more than two weeks longer than usual. During that period, Cape Canaveral received nearly four times the usual amount of rain, drenching the foam insulation around the 15-story external fuel tank, which helps lift the shuttle into orbit. According to NASA engineers, if rainwater had soaked into the insulation, which is applied as a foam and dries into a hard coating, it could have turned into a sizeable chunk of ice when the tank was filled with supercold liquid hydrogen and liquid oxygen the day before the launch.

The foam is exposed to incredible extremes in temperature. Before launch, as it keeps the 537,000 gallons of liquid fuel in the tank freezing cold, it must withstand temperatures as low as -423 degrees F. During launch, it must tolerate heat in excess of 1,200 degrees F. from the rocket exhaust and aerodynamic friction. The insulating foam is bound to the aluminum alloy fuel tank with a special epoxy cement, which has proven extremely durable. Chunks of insulation have been torn from the tank during numerous launches, but a strong layer always remains.

In 1997, a NASA decree to use more environmentally safe compounds resulted in a change in the insulation's formulation, possibly contributing to an increased rate of foam breakage during launch.

Also on February 4, NASA sent investigators to San Jose, California and Phoenix, Arizona to examine debris that witnesses said could have fallen from Columbia in the first moments of its breakup. At that point, there had been no confirmation that the shuttle lost any parts before it disintegrated over Texas, but Michael Kostelnik, head of NASA's shuttle and space station programs, said the reports were credible enough to warrant a look. "It's not clear what the material is," Kostelnik noted. "If it is wing material, it could be very important."

One of the reports came from Anthony Beasley, an astronomer at the California Institute of Technology's Owens Valley Radio Observatory east of Fresno. Beasley also told NASA officials that he had seen sudden flashes and objects trailing Columbia, as well as an instance in which something burning appeared to fall from the ship.

Investigators were hopeful because the discovery of thermal tiles or pieces of wing would help confirm the theory that Columbia's problems started almost immediately after it entered Earth's atmosphere. "If we found debris in California, Arizona or New Mexico along the ground path, certainly that would be a significant finding to us, and the particular debris would also point us in a direction," said Dittemore.

In addition to Beasley's reports, an amateur astronomer named Rick Baldridge photographed and videotaped Columbia as it passed over San Jose. Baldridge said his footage showed flares of light that appeared to be pieces of the shuttle breaking off.

During the February 4 press conference, NASA officials also disclosed that the agency was reviewing film of Columbia shot by a military helicopter as the shuttle flew across Texas. In total, NASA had received nearly 1,300 images of the doomed shuttle from eyewitnesses along its flight path.

On February 5, USA Today reported that on two earlier flights Columbia had experienced re-entry problems similar to those that occurred just before its destruction four days earlier. Quoting NASA records, the article noted that in each case, damage to heat-absorbing tiles on the shuttle's underside had affected the flow of air under the wings during re-entry. The result was excessive heat and additional stress on the damaged area.

Air flow and tile problems had come under NASA scrutiny before. In a report distributed during an international aeronautics meeting in October 2002, NASA scientists concluded that the issue needed prompt attention. Columbia's re-entry difficulties were specifically cited, though it was suggested that the problem affected all four shuttles in the NASA fleet.

The Columbia flights in question were STS-28 in 1989 and STS-73 in 1995. The NASA report described the 1995 re-entry as the one with the earliest onset of the airflow problems and the hottest entry recorded up to that date. It occurred at 13,000 miles per hour, which was highly unusual because shuttles typically don't experience airflow disruption until they slow to around 6,000 miles per hour.

The cause of the problems in the 1995 flight wasn't noted in the NASA report, though it did say that airflow problems are usually triggered by damage to grout-like material between the tiles. Such problems were first observed on the 1989 flight, during which a "rough surface" on the left wing caused airflow disruptions at 8,000 miles per hour.

To investigators, these two missions were particularly significant because they suggested a pattern of problems related to Columbia's left wing — the same wing that had recorded drag and temperature problems in the minutes before the shuttle fell apart. However, NASA officials still refused to say that tile damage from falling foam insulation was the definitive cause of the Columbia disaster, noting that they were still investigating other possible causes.

That the ongoing investigation was fluid and ever changing became clear February 5 when NASA officials started to back away from the falling foam theory as the primary cause of Columbia's destruction. During a press update, Ron Dittemore said that investigators strongly doubted that the chunk of red insulation could have set off the chain of events leading to the disaster. "We're looking somewhere else," Dittemore said. "It just doesn't make sense to us that a piece of debris would be the root cause of the loss of Columbia. There has to be another reason."

To prove his point, Dittemore displayed a chunk of insulation foam roughly the same size as the piece that struck Columbia. "It is very lightweight," he said. "It's not very hard. In fact, it's fragile. It's easy to break into particles."

Dittemore noted that investigators had enhanced the launch footage, which was fuzzy due to an incorrect camera setting, and concluded that it seemed to show no major damage where the insulation struck the wing.

Agency officials said they were also looking into the possibility that the underside of the shuttle had been struck by space debris or a micro-meteor sometime during its 16-day voyage.

More than a million pieces of "space junk," ranging in size from small bolts to satellites the size of cars, travel in Earth's orbit at incredible speed. Larger pieces are constantly tracked by the U.S. Air Force and shuttles are positioned to avoid them, but it's possible that a small piece — perhaps no larger than a man's thumb — struck Columbia's underside, damaging one or more of the ship's protective ceramic tiles and triggering a chain reaction when the ship entered the Earth's atmosphere.

There were, however, some flaws in the space debris theory. For one, the U.S. Air Force and NASA perform an analysis of the shuttle's orbit prior to liftoff to ensure that it will not encounter any foreign objects. And the analysis doesn't look only for large objects — the radar and optical monitoring are so precise that they can pinpoint the location of debris just a few inches in size.

Nonetheless, floating debris poses a hazard to every shuttle flight, and NASA has had to adjust the flight path of shuttles on at least eight occasions to avoid a collision.

Micro-debris — particles the size of a grain of sand — is also a potential hazard, but a very minimal one, experts say. In fact, researchers recently analyzed a craft that had been in space for five years and had been struck by micro-debris more than 30,000 times with no serious damage.

The investigation took an odd turn on February 6 when NASA Administrator Sean O'Keefe seemed to contradict Ron Dittemore by saying that the agency had not fully closed the door on the idea that falling foam insulation had ultimately doomed Columbia. O'Keefe asserted that only an independent panel had the authority to draw definitive conclusions.

There was also a challenge to Dittemore's claim that all of the engineers were in agreement that the shuttle was structurally sound for re-entry, despite being struck by the insulation. According to Knight Ridder reports, a key NASA supervisor said some engineers had expressed reservations about that conclusion.

Up to that point, Dittemore had solidly maintained that the only debate among engineers was over how to conduct an impact analysis of the damage caused by the falling debris. "These reservations were part of the process," said Dittemore, who characterized the issue as a normal debate between engineering disciplines. "In the end, when the question was asked: Are we satisfied that we have the right conclusion based on the analysis? Yes, we're satisfied."

But according to Knight Ridder, the supervisor said engineers had expressed serious concerns that the damage analysis conducted by Boeing Corp. wasn't reliable enough to conclude without doubt that the shuttle was unharmed. Dittemore was aware of those concerns, the supervisor added.

On February 8, NASA officials confirmed that Defense Department radar had shown an object or some material coming off Columbia as it orbited Earth a day after launch. Some researchers theorized that the signal represented a meteoroid impact, but NASA's spokesman in Houston, Kyle Herring, stressed that the space agency could not immediately gauge its significance. "The Department of Defense has provided the report to NASA, and we're assessing it," Herring said.

He added that investigators were looking closely at the shuttle's inflight schedule to determine whether the debris might have come from a routine dump of waste or other supplies. At the same time, they were examining data from instruments aboard the craft that might have registered a sudden vibration that could have resulted from impact with a foreign body.

Meanwhile, in Washington, Steven Wallace, a member of the Columbia Accident Investigation Board, told the Washington Post that the body had no time table for drawing conclusions, and that the investigation would take as long as necessary. "There is no timeline," said Wallace. "The number one priority is to get it right."

Wallace stressed that every piece of evidence would be analyzed and that nothing would be ruled out until the board was absolutely certain it knew what caused Columbia to disintegrate.

By then an entire week had passed since Columbia's demise, and NASA officials were no closer to definitive answers than they had been at the beginning. Frustration was setting in as investigators hit one dead end after another and every new piece of information posed more questions than it answered. Most depressing was that even the simplest of technologies seemed to have failed at a time when they were needed the most. The camera aimed at Columbia's left wing, for example, was so out of focus that the footage was almost worthless. And analysts were having a difficult time making sense of the flight data gathered during the shuttle's final minutes.

The Columbia tragedy was proving far more difficult to solve than the Challenger disaster. In that case, scientists were pretty certain within hours of the explosion that they knew what had happened, though the investigation and final report would take many months to complete.

With Columbia, patience, discipline and a whole lot of luck would obviously be the keys to success.

Fearful of missing obvious clues, investigators began assembling what engineers call "fault trees" — a chain of possible causes that would have to be studied one by one. "Let me emphasize again that we have not ruled out any possible cause," Dittemore told reporters during a briefing several days following the accident. "You have to look at each branch, each block, each possible cause, to determine that you have done a thorough job."

On February 9, the investigation took a new direction when NASA officials reported that they were studying the possibility that Columbia may have been damaged by a large chunk of ice that formed on a wastewater vent. The opening is located under the shuttle cabin in front of the left wing, and is used to expel urine and surplus water generated by the shuttle's fuel cells. The water usually shoots into space as harmless crystals, but on a 1984 Discovery mission it formed into a large block on the lip of the vent. During that mission, the astronauts used the ship's robotic arm to break off the ice so it wouldn't damage the shuttle during re-entry.

Just one day after Columbia's launch, the U.S. Space Command of the Air Force, which routinely monitors objects in space, detected an object moving quickly away from the shuttle. It was assumed to have come from the ship, and was most likely a chunk of ice, said Adm. Hal Gehman, head of the investigation board. He added: "These reports are emerging. It's too early to say if they mean anything."

NASA engineers said that if ice had accumulated on the wastewater vent, it could have slammed into the left wing during re-entry, damaging some of the thermal tiles.

During the February 9 press briefing, NASA Administrator Sean O'Keefe also reported that searchers had found a two-foot piece of wing with attached thermal tiles, the 300-pound cover of a landing gear compartment and what appeared to be a hatch door with a hydraulic opening and closing mechanism. Those pieces and the thousands of others collected so far were scheduled to be shipped to the Kennedy Space Center, where investigators planned to reassemble as much of the ship as possible.

The next day, NASA officials revealed that the shuttle fleet did not have sensors along the leading edges of the ships' wings to detect collisions with debris or warn of extreme temperatures that could endanger the ship during re-entry. Columbia did have such sensors when it was introduced in 1981, but they were removed because engineers did not believe they would be particularly useful and eliminating them reduced the weight of the ship. Lack of wing-edge sensors could explain why the shuttle's astronauts apparently had no idea the orbiter was in trouble until it began to break apart during re-entry.

Meanwhile, Michael Kostelnik confirmed that engineers were examining high-resolution photographs of Columbia taken by an Air Force telescope camera. One photo, taken just moments before the shuttle disintegrated, showed a dark gray streak trailing the left wing, and the leading edge of that wing appeared to be jagged.

In addition, human remains had been discovered in a Texas farmer's field, along with gauges and other components. And at the Toledo Bend Reservoir near the Texas-Louisiana border, divers retrieved a 40-pound chunk of metal, though officials were unable to immediately identify it.

On February 11, NASA released the audio tapes of the final communications between ground controllers and the crew. They showed that Jeff Kling, the Maintenance and Mechanical Officer at Mission Control who was monitoring Columbia's descent, noticed the loss of data from temperature gauges about eight minutes before all communication was lost. Flight Director Leroy Cain sounded surprised but not particularly alarmed by the news. He asked Kling if the sensors had gone out at the same time. "No, not exactly," Kling replied. "They were within probably four or five seconds of each other."

A few moments later, Cain reported drag on the craft, but controllers thought it was handling okay. "Control's been stable through the rolls that we've done so far flying," said Navigation Officer Mike Sarafin as Columbia approached the Arizona-New Mexico border. "We have good trims. I don't see anything out of the ordinary."

Also on February 11, the three crewmen of the International Space Station — NASA astronauts Ken Bowersox and Don Pettit, and Russian cosmonaut Nikolai Budarin — broke their public silence to say that the isolation of space had made it difficult for them to cope with the loss of their colleagues. "When you're up here this long, you can't just bottle up your emotions and cope with it all the time," said Bowersox during a teleconference. "It's important for us to acknowledge that the people on (Columbia) were our friends. We feel their loss."

In addition to losing close friends and colleagues, the space station crew had also lost their ride home when Columbia went down. As a result, their four-month tour in space could conceivably last more than a year.

The following day, February 12, NASA Administrator Sean O'Keefe appeared before a joint House-Senate hearing in Washington to defend the Columbia Accident Investigation Board. Lawmakers said they were skeptical that the board would be able to act with "full independence."

O'Keefe strongly defended the integrity of the inquiry board, and assured legislators that the cause of the accident would be found. However, Rep. Sherwood Boehlert, chairman of the House Science Committee, called for an enlargement of the board, which many lawmakers felt was too heavy with past and current government officials. Boehlert expressed skepticism of the inquiry board's "independence and latitude."

Meanwhile, it was revealed that flight controllers in Houston had received e-mail messages during Columbia's mission from a NASA engineer who outlined a horrifying scenario in which a tire might explode, producing "carnage in the wheel well" and a possible disaster when the shuttle returned from orbit.

Robert Daugherty, who worked in NASA's Langley facility in Hampton, Virginia, sent the e-mail to a colleague at the Johnson Space Center on January 30, two days before Columbia was destroyed during re-entry. Daugherty wrote that if there were a heat shield failure in the area of the wheel well, "at some point the wheel could fail and send debris everywhere . . .with that much carnage in the wheel well, something could get screwed up enough to prevent deployment and then you are in a world of hurt."

The e-mail messages were the first known documentation that someone at NASA had outlined a specific scenario during the mission in which damage to the heat shield could lead to a catastrophe. However, NASA officials downplayed the messages, calling them part of a routine "what if?" process that flight controllers are encouraged to engage in as part of their training and preparation for crisis.

On February 13, the investigation board reported that a hole might have developed in Columbia's skin that allowed incredibly hot gases to flow into the left wing, resulting in the ship's destruction.

"Preliminary analysis by a NASA working group . . . indicates that the temperature indications seen in Columbia's left wheel well during entry would require the presence of plasma," the superheated gas that surrounds the shuttle during re-entry, said the board in a statement released to the press. "The heat transfer through the structure, as from a missing tile, would not be sufficient to cause the temperature indications seen in the last minutes of the flight." Instead, the board said, only a jet of plasma — which can reach temperatures of 3,000 degrees F. as a result of atmospheric friction — could have caused the heating and equipment failures detected shortly before Columbia crashed.

Still unexplained was how the hole was created or exactly where it may have been located. Possibilities included the fuselage, on the surface of the left wing or on its leading edge, through the seal of the wheel well or directly through the door of the wheel well, said NASA spokesman James Hartsfield, adding, "The engineering teams are optimistic that they can continue the reverse engineering they've been working on, and narrow down the possibilities."

The catastrophic implications of such a breach, whether from falling insulation or space debris, were discussed in a 1997 report from the National Research Council, which stated: "Impacts that penetrate the leading edge of the wing or the lower surfaces of the wing or the fuselage might not be immediately critical or even detected, but the consequent thermal heating on re-entry could have a 'blow torch' effect inside the wing that causes loss of flight control or failure of the preliminary structure resulting in the loss of the vehicle. Major damage to the control surfaces or the hydraulic systems that operate them could result in critical failure during re-entry, approach and landing."

During the February 13 press briefing, NASA also released a detailed map illustrating for the first time that the shuttle's sensors had started detecting very subtle signs of trouble when the ship was still over the Pacific Ocean, about 400 miles off the coast of California — far earlier than initially believed.

While NASA investigators struggled to determine the cause of the Columbia disaster, the world asked what, if anything, could have been done to identify the problem while the ship was still in space, or to save the crew during re-entry.

Foremost was the question of why a space walk wasn't performed to inspect the exterior of the shuttle if there was even a slight possibility that something had damaged the heat tiles during launch. The answer is two-fold. First, NASA officials had witnessed insulation break off and strike tiles in earlier launches, so this was not a new phenomenon. But more importantly, video footage of this particular strike strongly suggested that no serious damage had occurred, so engineers saw no reason for a space-walk inspection.

But even if such an inspection had been warranted, there was no way that the crew of STS-107 could have performed it. For one thing, such a maneuver requires special equipment that was not available. More importantly, a walk of this nature would have been so dangerous as to be suicidal because there is nothing under the wing to hold on to. Without the aid of jet packs, the astronauts would have had no way to return to the ship.

The point is moot anyway, because even if damaged tiles had been located and the astronauts had been able to access them, a repair of this type is impossible in space. Attaching the special ceramic tiles is far more complicated than simply laying down some glue and slapping them on; it's a multi-step process that requires specific tools and materials.

Connecting with the International Space Station to make repairs was also out of the question. Flying the shuttle is not like driving a car: you can't just point it in a particular direction and hit the accelerator. Columbia was in an orbit which did not intersect with the ISS, and altering its course would have required more fuel than could be spared. In addition, Columbia was the one ship in the fleet that did not make routine flights to the space station and thus did not have the proper docking system. So, even if the craft had been able to reach the station, the astronauts would have had no way of getting inside.

Others questioned the possibility of the crew ejecting during re-entry once it became obvious that the ship was in serious trouble. Interestingly, as the first shuttle in the fleet, Columbia was equipped with two ejection seats during its test phase - one for the commander and one for the pilot. However, the ejection seats were removed and the explosive roof panels replaced once the number of crew members on each mission started to climb.

There is a contingency for the crew to bail out under certain circumstances, but rapid ejection (the kind used by fighter pilots) from a space shuttle simply isn't feasible. Half of the crew is sitting on the ship's mid-deck during launch and re-entry, making ejection for them impossible. And the idea of leaving even one crew member behind in an emergency is unthinkable to any astronaut. Even if rapid ejection had been possible, Columbia was flying too high and too fast at the time she fell apart for anyone to have survived.

Chapter 3
Seven into Space

Anyone who has ever met an astronaut will tell you there's something that makes them unique, a little larger than life. Each member of Columbia's final crew was like that. Although many had families, mortgages and car payments just like the rest of us, they were not only willing, but eager to put their lives on the line for the betterment of humanity. From the time that Yuri Gagarin and Alan Shepherd first shook off the bonds of Earth and ascended on chariots of fire to the cold void above, it was obvious that these spacefarers were cut from the toughest of cloth.

The seven souls who boarded Columbia on a cool January day were not heroes in their own minds — far from it. They were just doing their jobs, as they had done for years while preparing for flight. But the specter of disaster was always there, just over their shoulders, although somehow they were able to proceed as if it wasn't.

With their passing, the world lost seven extremely accomplished and extraordinary men and women, but their spirit of exploration and desire to expand the boundaries of man's knowledge could not — and has not — died with them.

Here are their stories.

✳ Rick Husband ✳
Mission Commander

Rick Husband's life goal had been clear since he was a little boy. "From the time I was about four years old, I wanted to be an astronaut. It was about that time that the Mercury program first started up. I saw those things on the TV, and it just really excited me," he once recalled.

"And for the whole time I was growing up, for as long as I can remember, any time anyone asked me what I wanted to be it was, 'I want to be an astronaut.'" At the time, other kids in his Amarillo, Texas neighborhood laughed at Husband's dream. "Not necessarily that they thought it was funny, but that at such a young age he'd already decided what he wanted to be," explained Bob Stewart, a former neighbor.

The young Husband recalled being elated when the first plastic space models began appearing in stores. "I remember building a Gemini model. From Mercury to Gemini to Apollo, watching the moon landings and everything, it was just so incredibly adventurous and exciting to me that I just thought, 'There is no doubt in my mind that that's what I want to do when I grow up.'"

Husband graduated from high school in Amarillo in 1975 and learned to fly when he was 18. He earned a bachelor's degree in mechanical engineering from Texas Tech University in 1980. "If you wanted to draw a picture of an all-American boy, that would be Rick," recalled Dr. James Lawrence, a Texas Tech engineering professor.

When Husband heard that NASA was looking for astronauts, he was immediately interested, but had no idea what it took to become one. "So I sent a letter off to NASA asking them what kind of requirements were necessary to become an astronaut," he recalled. "I got a package back telling me about the pilots and mission specialists and the requirements that were necessary."

With the path to outer space now clearly marked, Husband began training as an Air Force pilot at Vance Air Force Base in Oklahoma. He flew F-4 Phantom jets and F-15 Strike Eagles, and eventually became a flight instructor. In 1987, he became a test pilot after attending the U.S. Air Force Test Pilot school and earned a master's degree in 1990. With all of NASA's requirements fulfilled, Husband applied to the astronaut office — only to be turned down.

"I applied four different times," said Husband, "and interviewed two different times, and then was hired after the second interview. It was the achievement of a lifelong dream. And it's very humbling, I'd say, and exciting to be able to go and actually do the thing I'd wanted to do, and the thing that I had looked forward to doing for such a long time."

By the time he was accepted for astronaut training in 1994, Husband had more than 3,800 hours of flight time in more than 40 types of aircraft. After five years of preparation and training for the space program, he rode Discovery into orbit in 1999 on the flight of STS-96. Husband was in the pilot's seat when Shuttle Commander Kent Rominger successfully steered the shuttle to the first docking with the new International Space Station. On that mission, Husband brought with him a Texas Tech T-shirt and a medallion bearing the school's mechanical engineering logo. The T-shirt, signed by the Discovery crew, and the medallion, are now on display at the school.

When it was time to undock from the Space Station, Husband finally got a chance to fly Discovery. "We had the opportunity to do two and a half revolutions of the space station while

I was flying the orbiter," he recalled. "And I remember during that one time, when we were doing that fly-around, about somewhere in the middle of it I just finally turned around and looked at everybody and said 'This is so much fun!'"

Although he had just one space mission under his belt, Husband was chosen to command Columbia on STS-107. Just days before the January 16 launch, Husband said, "It's been pretty much a lifelong dream and just a thrill to be able to get to actually live it."

Husband lived in Lubbock with his wife Evelyn, their 8-year-old daughter Lauren and son Matthew, 3. A talented baritone, Husband still sang in church choirs. He loved water skiing, snow skiing and biking. Neighbor Elsa Klein, who attended Houston's Grace Community Church with the Husband family, said, "I can't think of a better father or a finer Christian."

In a Today Show interview, Husband's widow Evelyn remembered her husband being much more nervous about his first flight into space than the Columbia mission. "The first time he flew he was much more uptight than this time," she said. "This time I wasn't concerned. He loved to fly — this is the ultimate experience." Husband knew that space travel was a dangerous business, Evelyn said, adding: "It was important to him that our family remain intact and be strong."

In an interview shortly before Columbia's last mission, Husband showed how deep his love for his family and a Higher Power ran: "If I ended up at the end of my life having been an astronaut but having sacrificed my family along the way, or living my life in a way that didn't glorify God, then I would look back on it with great regret."

✳ William C. McCool ✳ Pilot

Like many astronauts, Willie McCool fell in love with building model airplanes as a child — an early clue that flying would be his life's work. And for McCool, piloting Columbia exceeded all his dreams.

"It's beyond imagination," McCool — a former test pilot and commander in the U.S. Navy — told National Public Radio in a broadcast from Columbia. "Until you actually get up and see it and experience it and feel it . . . I'll tell you, there's nothing better than listening to a good album and looking out the windows and watching the world go by while you pedal on the (exercise) bike."

McCool was born in San Diego. His father, Vietnam veteran Barry McCool, was a Marine infantryman who later became a Navy aviator, so McCool attended junior high school in Guam before moving to Lubbock, Texas. "My father — prior military, Marine and Naval aviator — had a big influence on me," he says. "As a child he was a big advocate of building model airplanes, so I had this natural inclination for flying. I went to the Naval Academy and into Naval aviation in my father's footsteps and as my career progressed, things just worked out in my benefit to lead me into the astronaut program."

A 1979 graduate of Lubbock's Coronado High School, he's remembered fondly by many. Ed Jarman, McCool's chemistry teacher, recalls: "Willie had one of the best senses of humor of any kid you'd ever seen. He could always see the humor in anything. Instead of Willie McCool, everyone called him Cool Willie." Coronado classmate Tricia Burcham remembered McCool as "very popular, athletic and extremely smart. He was friends with everybody," while Dale Somers, a high school friend, said, "he was dedicated in everything he did. He was all-out all the time."

McCool also excelled at sports. In 1978, the year before he graduated, he competed in a three-mile race. Among the other contestants was a runner named George W. Bush. The future astronaut burned up the track, finishing first in about 16 minutes, while the future

President crossed the finish line somewhere back in the middle of the pack.

After high school, McCool went on to attend the U.S. Naval Academy, where he ran with the cross-country team and placed second in his class of 1,083. At the Academy, he earned two master's degrees — one in computer science and another in aeronautical engineering — while continuing to pursue his dream of flying.

"I loved the idea of flying jets, so I thought I would go into aviation," McCool said. "Test pilot school would be fun. I'll go there. Things just fell into place." He got his wings as a fighter pilot in 1986 and was assigned to an electronic warfare squadron. While in the Navy, he served two tours of duty in the Mediterranean aboard the aircraft carrier USS Coral Sea. After logging more than 2,800 flight hours, he was chosen for NASA's astronaut program in 1996 while serving on the USS Enterprise as a squadron administrative and operations officer. McCool boarded Columbia with a piece of his hometown — a spirit towel for the Coronado Mustangs.

Remembering how much the influence and support of his father and other adults meant to him, McCool was a huge supporter of using the shuttle for student experiments, as they did on STS-107. "Most of what we're doing now is enabling technology for the future," he said, "and the folks who are going to use that technology and then continue the wheel turning are the children today. And I'll tell you what: there's just no greater experience, at least in my career thus far, than to see the excitement and the eyes that light up when you talk to kids about experiments. And when they really get a chance to go hands-on with them — boy! — yeah, the wheels really started turning! The fires get going. And it's just a great opportunity to foster that experience for them."

A runner, swimmer and back-country camper, McCool relaxed by playing the guitar and chess. He and his wife Atilana, known as Lani, lived in Lubbock with their three sons.

Although it is not well known, all astronauts are asked to choose a representative to sit on an investigative panel should they be killed in the line of duty. McCool picked his father. The man Willie idolized will work closely with the investigative team in the months to come as the jigsaw puzzle that was once Columbia is painstakingly reassembled to determine why his son and the rest of the crew died in the skies over Texas. Hopefully, he will find closure and help make sure that other lives are not similarly lost.

✳ Michael P. Anderson ✳
Payload Commander

Michael Anderson got his first toy airplane at age 3, and from then on he not only dreamed of flying in space, he planned on it. A fan of the Star Trek and Lost in Space television shows, he built moon homes for his sister Brenda's Barbie dolls. As a 9-year-old who knew the names of the astronauts who landed on the moon, he could barely contain his excitement as he watched them do it. Brenda recalled him shouting from the top bunk, "Let's go to the moon!" as they pretended their bunk bed was a spaceship.

His mother Barbara remembered her son as "always different from most kids. When everybody else was off playing, he was inside doing experiments with his chemistry sets or studying some sort of electronics." Anderson's interest in science was so pervasive that high school science teacher Hal Sautter remembered Anderson as a "lab rat." With that kind of dedication, it's no wonder the young student grew up to be an astronaut. "I can't remember ever thinking that I couldn't do it," Anderson, a lieutenant colonel in the U.S. Air Force, said in an interview. "I never had any serious doubts about it. It was just a matter of when."

Anderson was born on Christmas Day 1959 in Plattsburgh, N.Y. and grew up near Spokane, Washington, after his father, an Air Force serviceman, was assigned to Fairchild Air Force Base. He attended school in Cheney, a farm town next to the base. "He was a very gentle, determined young man," said Rev. Happy Watkins, who taught Anderson's Sunday school class.

After graduating from Cheney High School, Anderson earned a bachelor of science degree in physics and astronomy from the University of Washington. He followed his father's footsteps into the Air Force, then earned a master's in physics at Creighton University in Omaha, Nebraska. With his sights set firmly on the space program, Anderson carefully chose which aircraft to fly in order to maximize his chances of becoming an astronaut.

"One day I said, 'Well, you know, I've been flying airplanes here in the Air Force for quite some time now, and I have a record there. And I studied science in school. And I'm really ready to put together a package and send it off to NASA and see what they think.' And fortunately, I got called down for an interview. And one thing led to the next, and one day I got that call."

The call came in 1994, proving that all of his hard work, planning and persistence had paid off. Out of 2,962 applicants, Anderson was one of only 19 candidates to be chosen. His first space flight was aboard Endeavor in 1998, which docked with the Russian space station Mir. STS-89 was the eighth Shuttle-Mir docking mission, and during their 10-day stay the crew transferred more than 9,000 pounds of scientific equipment, logistical hardware and water from the space shuttle to Mir. In the fifth and last exchange of a U.S. astronaut, STS-89 brought astronaut Andy Thomas up to Mir and ferried David Wolf back to Earth.

During that mission, Anderson became the first African-American to visit a space station, a distinction he downplayed. "I hadn't really thought about it," he said. "Any time you break ground on something new, there's some benefit." But he took pride in being a role model for children because he enjoyed doing "anything I can to inspire a young child, to tell someone about the importance of education." Anderson lived in Clear Lake City, Texas with his wife Sandra and their two daughters. According to his official NASA biography, he enjoyed photography, chess, computers and tennis. On Columbia, Anderson was in charge of science experiments.

While he recognized the value of the space mission, he didn't ignore the dangers. "When you launch in a rocket, you're not really flying that rocket, you're just hanging on," he said. "You're taking an explosion and trying to harness that energy in a way that will propel you into space. And we're very successful in doing that. But even though we've gone to great pains to make it as safe as we can, there's always the potential for something going wrong. There's always that unknown. And

I guess it's that unknown that I don't like."

Nevertheless, despite his aversion to liftoffs and landings, Anderson never second-guessed his career choice. "I take the risk because I think what we're doing is really important," he said. "For me, it's the fact that what I'm doing can have great consequences and great benefits for everyone, for mankind."

During a memorial service at Anderson's church in Spokane, Washington, pastor Freeman Simmons recalled a conversation he had with Anderson shortly before Columbia's demise. "He always wanted to fly," said Simmons. "He told me, 'If this thing doesn't come out right, don't worry about me. I'm just going on higher.' He was an eagle."

Childhood friend Eva Millan said that Anderson's faith prepared him for anything: "He believed when he was up in space he was that much closer to God if anything happened."

✳ Kalpana Chawla ✳
Mission Specialist 2

Kalpana Chawla was in 10th grade when she decided to become an aerospace engineer. Her father scoffed at her, suggesting she become a doctor or teacher instead. "Those were more respectable professions," recalled Chawla, a certified flight instructor.

She was born in Karna, India, a small town about 75 miles north of New Delhi. From a very early age she was interested in flight, and recalled watching planes fly and wishing she could be in them. "When I was going to high school back in India, we lived in a very small town that had a flying club," she recalled. "And we would see these small Pushpak airplanes, not much different from Piper J3 Cubs that you see U.S. students fly as part of their training programs. Me and my brother, sometimes we would be on bikes looking up, trying to see where these airplanes were headed. My dad took us to the flying club and got us a ride in the Pushpak and a glider. I think that's really my closest link to aerospace engineering."

Chawla grew up a devout Hindu and vegetarian. Upon applying to Punjab Engineering College, the dean tried to steer her away from her dream, but Chawla stood firm. "I will stay if you are giving me admission in aeronautics, otherwise I'll go home," she told him. Chawla stayed and earned an engineering degree from Punjab in 1982, then set her sights on an education that would send her into space. Even when her father Banarsi Lal, a self-made man who owned a rubber manufacturing plant, discouraged her plans, warning that holding an advanced degree would hurt her chances of finding a husband, Chawla was undeterred.

However, India did not have an aerospace program, and it became obvious the young woman would have to emigrate in order to follow her dream. "I was interested in aerospace and flying, and the U.S. is really the best place in the world for flying," she told the University of Texas at Arlington Magazine in 1998.

Her plans to emigrate scandalized her parents' friends and relatives in Karna. "How can you send your unmarried daughter abroad alone?" they gasped. One relative even suggested the parents try hard to marry their daughter off before she left for America. Finally, realizing that she was not to be dissuaded, Chawla's parents asked her brother Sanjay to escort her to the United States and make sure she was safe as she found a place to live and settled down. "She's an adventurous girl who never wastes time," said Sanjay. "I had no doubts that she would scale heights in the future."

Chawla went on to earn a master's degree in aerospace engineering at the University of Texas, and a doctorate at the University of Colorado. Along the way, she became an American citizen and met Jean-Pierre Harrison, a freelance flying instructor. The young woman was smitten, and the two married in 1984. Inspired by her husband's career, she began taking flying lessons and obtained her pilot's license in 1987. "I like airplanes, it's that simple," she said. "Flying, for me, is sheer fun. It appeals to all my senses."

NASA selected Chawla for the astronaut program in 1994. Like her final shuttle mission, Chawla's first in 1997 on STS-87 was a 16-day marathon science mission on Columbia. One of her responsibilities on that flight was to deploy a 3,000-pound satellite called Spartan, which was to fly free of the shuttle to examine the sun's corona. After Chawla deployed the satellite using Columbia's robotic arm, it was supposed to begin rotating for stability, but instead it remained stationary. When she attempted to retrieve it with the arm, the satellite began to oscillate, making recovery impossible. After deliberation, NASA mission controllers came up with a plan. With Chawla's help on the robot arm, astronauts Winston Scott and Takao Doi, firmly tethered to Columbia, were able to grab the balky satellite and wrestle it into the ship's cargo bay.

The flight marked the first space trip by an Indian-born woman, and residents in her hometown stayed up late to watch video of the mission on TV and celebrate with a torchlight procession. Chawla was flattered, but humble. "For me, it's really far-fetched to have thought about it and made it," she said. "I never truly thought about being the first or second someone, or being the small-town girl. This is just something I wanted to do. It was very important for me to enjoy it. It's almost like having won the lottery or something."

Interestingly, Chawla's ambitions while in college did not extend to becoming an astronaut, as she recalled in an interview on the eve of the STS-107 launch: "If people asked me what I wanted to do, I remember in the first year I would say, 'I want to be a flight engineer.' But I am quite sure at that time I didn't really have a good idea of what a flight engineer did, because flight engineers do not do aircraft design, which was an area I wanted to pursue and did pursue in my career. And it's sort of a nice coincidence that that's what I am doing on this flight."

On STS-107, Chawla was enthralled by the gorgeous views of Earth she saw from the shuttle, and described her impressions to an interviewer: "Earth is very beautiful. I wish everyone could see it. The Ganges River looked majestic, mind-boggling. You see the continents go by, the thunderstorms shimmering in the clouds, the city lights at night."

Ironically, Chawla landed a spot on Columbia because of her petite size. "She was very small, maybe 5 feet if that, and NASA had no suits for extra-vehicular activities that fit her," said Robert Culp, a professor at the University of Colorado who was Chawla's mentor. "That was why she was on the Columbia. It does not go to the International Space Station, where you need the special suits." By the end of Columbia's last flight, Chawla had racked up an astounding 6.5 million miles in space.

Although she had become an American citizen, Chawla was a role model to many in India. "After her first flight, she became a national hero," said R.S. Bhatia of the Indian Space Research Organization, India's equivalent to NASA. "She is an American citizen, but she is ours too. This is the most terrible tragedy. We have lost a hero."

✳ David M. Brown ✳
Mission Specialist 1

"I always let him dream." That's what Dot Brown said about her son David, whose dreams were as big as the universe.

"I remember growing up thinking astronauts and their job was the coolest thing you could possibly do," said Brown, a captain in the U.S. Navy and a flight surgeon. "I thought they were movie stars."

Dubbed "the accidental astronaut" in an article published by his alma mater, the College of William and Mary, Brown took an unusual path to the heavens. A star gymnast at Yorktown High School in Virginia, he joined the circus while in college. He juggled, pedaled a 7-foot tall unicycle and walked on stilts while majoring in biology. Before enrolling in Eastern Virginia Medical School, he spent a year flying over the western United States and Alaska with a friend.

"That's how Dave's life went," said Cliff Gauthier, a gymnastics coach at William and Mary. "He always pursued his dreams. He jumped on opportunities when he got them." While attending medical school, a Navy pamphlet changed his life. "I got a brochure that showed a Navy physician standing on a flight deck next to an F-4 Phantom," Brown recalled. "I said, 'Boy, I've got to go learn about this.'"

And so he did. After graduating from medical school, he joined the Navy and was assigned to a Navy hospital in Alaska. He then served on the aircraft carrier USS Carl Vinson, earning the title of Navy Operational Flight Surgeon of the Year in 1986. Working on airplanes whetted his appetite to learn to fly. In 1988, he became the only Navy physician in a 10-year period to be chosen for flight training. "The first time I applied they said, 'No, you're not going to do that'," Brown recalled. "I thought about it and said, 'Well, I really would like to do this.' So I reapplied and they said, 'Yes.'"

Two years later Brown graduated first in his flight school class and was assigned to the Naval Strike Warfare Center in Nevada. In 1992, he spent a stint aboard the aircraft carrier USS Independence, then began a tour of duty as a flight surgeon at the U.S. Naval Test Pilot School in 1995 where he began applying to be an astronaut. His love of flight was so great that Brown once told friends, "Some people dream of living on a golf course — my dream is to live on an airstrip, where I can come home and fly."

He was chosen for the astronaut program in 1996 on his third try. Hooked on space, he kept a telescope in his Houston living room pointed at the moon, and was excited about his upcoming first trip into space. "The greatest thing about being an astronaut is you get to do a little bit of everything," he said. "We're going to ride a rocket uphill. We're going to have the most amazing views of the Earth. And at the same time, we get to participate in fundamental research that will contribute to medical understanding, physical sciences understanding, and a better understanding of the Earth and the Earth's atmosphere."

On the flight Brown carried a small flag from his alma mater, Yorktown High School in Virginia, which he had attended along with Katie Couric, co-host of NBC's Today Show. The flag had been carried to the summit of Mount Everest by a fellow alumnus, and in an interview before the flight Brown joked, "I'm going to get it a little bit higher up, but I won't have to walk as far to get it there." When informed of Brown's death by a Today

Show producer, Couric had to struggle to fight back tears.

A bachelor, Brown's closest companion was Duggins, his yellow Labrador Retriever. When he moved into a development built around an airstrip in 1996, Brown became friends with the neighboring Swindell family, who would often take care of Duggins while Brown was in training. "He and Duggins became part of our family and we became part of his," said Cindy Swindell. About a year and a half ago, the 15-year-old Lab became ill with cancer. While Brown was preparing for the mission, the dog's suffering became unbearable and the Swindells were forced to have him put to sleep, just two days before Columbia's liftoff.

When Cindy called Brown at the Kennedy Space Center and informed him of the loss, "Dave was very understanding and said to do what I had to do," she remembered. "He was more interested in comforting me than me comforting him about his lovable dog. The man loses his best friend, and he is still able to think about others. And that was my last conversation with him. He said he was so excited about the mission he couldn't even sleep. I'm just glad he got the chance to live his life's dream."

Thrilled at being chosen to fly on Columbia, Brown shared his accomplishment by inviting friends to attend the January 16 launch. "He sent tickets to neighbors and friends who had followed his career since 1982," said Dr. Gordon Iiams, Brown's roommate for two years during medical school. "They loved him."

✳ Laurel Clark ✳
Mission Specialist 4

Whether it was scuba diving or rock climbing, mountain hiking or parachuting, Laurel Clark never shied from a challenge. A classic overachiever, the Columbia Mission Specialist had also been a Navy commander, a pediatrician and a flight surgeon who studied zoology and undersea medicine by the time she took to the skies on the space shuttle. "Laurel was never one of these people to say, 'OK, I found what I want to do.' It was always, 'What's the next challenge?'" said her younger brother, Daniel Salton. "She was one of these people who had a goal, saw the goal, the end result and knew how much work it would take to get there and was willing to do it."

"She never had a lot of failures, I can tell you that," said her father, Robert Salton.

And as a crew member on Columbia, Clark had achieved the goal of a lifetime. Clark was born in Iowa, but grew up in Racine, Wisconsin which she considered her hometown. The oldest of four siblings, she could be a handful. "In about fifth grade, I stopped trying to argue with her about things I wanted her to do because she could always win the argument," said her dad. "She always had logic on her side."

Bill Frayer, one of Clark's teachers at Horlick High School in Racine, remembers her drive and ambition: "It was obvious from early on that Laurel was a special individual who'd go on to achieve great things."

An animal lover, Clark majored in zoology at the University of Wisconsin in Madison. She intended to become a veterinarian, but attended medical school there instead. Next, she spent 10 years in the Navy, earning her certification to work in submarines and as a medical diver. NASA accepted her for astronaut training in 1996, although going into space had never been one of her goals.

"I can't think of anything specific growing up that pointed me toward NASA at all," Clark said. "I was interested in the moon landings just about the same as everyone else of my generation. But I never really thought about being an astronaut or working in space myself." But once she focused on NASA as a career, she threw herself into it wholeheartedly. "When I learned about NASA and what astronauts do, I thought about the things I'd done so far and became more interested," she confessed.

A flight surgeon and Naval commander with three Navy commendation medals, Clark married her husband Jonathan, a neurologist who also served in the Navy, in 1991. The couple had an 8-year-old son, Iain.

Though Clark and her family had suffered a tremendous loss in September 2001 when her cousin, Timothy Haviland, died in the attack on the World Trade Center, Clark's brother Daniel confessed that he never thought about her safety even though going into space is always a risk — until he watched the shuttle launch first-hand. "I was just an emotional wreck when she was in space, when you actually see that rocket go up," he said. "Visions of the Challenger go through your head and you pray that it's not going to happen. Once they're up in space, big sigh of relief — 'OK, the dangerous part is over.' I never even considered that something could happen on the way down."

While in space, Clark had sent an inspiring email to her family and friends, describing the awesome sights she had seen through Columbia's windows, including her Wisconsin home town: "I feel blessed to be here representing our country and carrying out the research of scientists around the world. Magically, the very first day, we flew over Lake Michigan and I saw Wind Point, Wisconsin clearly. Whenever I get to look out, it's glorious. Even the stars have a special brightness."

At mission's end, Clark moved to the rear center seat on the flight deck in the role of Flight Engineer for the de-orbit burn and re-entry. "I have a computer screen back near my seat where I can monitor the overall health of the vehicle and pick up any problems that might be occurring early on, or once we see any kind of a malfunction or anything unusual that's happening, we can look at the data and figure out what that is," Clark explained. "Of course, we trained for a lot more malfunctions than any ever happen. So most of the time you don't have to do much, other than monitor the normal entry profile." Tragically, Columbia's re-entry was anything but routine.

In a CNN interview, Daniel Clark noted that his sister was never satisfied with just "good enough," but was driven to always do her absolute best in any endeavor. "Laurel was a very intense person who would set goals and would go for them," he said. "And I think that's a great role model for kids today, to know that the goal-oriented stuff that they talk about, that the counselors in school tell you about — it works. It gets you places. You can do great things for humanity if you just set some small goals and always go for the next thing and set your sights higher."

✴ Ilan Ramon ✴
Payload Specialist

Ilan Ramon was 16 when a neighbor took him for a ride in his small Cessna airplane. Remembered childhood friend Ronit Segelman, "Flying was one of the things Ilan loved to do more than anything. For him, it was just a way of life. It was his profession."

Ramon was well aware of the historic importance of being the first Israeli to go into space. "To be the first Israeli astronaut is symbolic for all Israelis," Ramon said before Columbia's launch on January 16. "My mother is a Holocaust survivor. She was in Auschwitz. My father fought for the independence of Israel not so long ago. I was born in Israel and I'm kind of the proof for them, and for the whole Israeli people, that whatever we fought for and we've been going through in the last century — or maybe in the last two thousand years — is becoming true.

"I was talking to a lot of, for instance, Holocaust survivors. And when you talk to these people who are pretty old today, and you tell them that you're going to be in space as an Israeli astronaut, they look at you as a dream that they could never have dreamed of. So it is very exciting for me to be able to fulfill their dream that they wouldn't dare to dream."

Ramon grew up in a Tel Aviv suburb. He graduated from high school in 1972, and like all other young Israelis, was compelled to enter military service. Ramon attended the Israel Air Force Flight School, and after graduation followed his dream of becoming a fighter pilot, logging more than 4,000 hours in high-performance combat jets, including the F-16 Fighting Falcon. "Flying fighter aircraft is great," Ramon said, "and I love to fly!"

A veteran of the 1973 Yom Kippur war and the 1982 Israeli invasion of Lebanon, Ramon was already a war hero when he took part in the 1981 raid that destroyed Iraq's unfinished nuclear reactor at Osirak near Baghdad. He and seven other pilots flew in low, their F-16s hugging the ground to evade enemy radar, and completely destroyed the reactor, which was considered a strategic threat to the Jewish state. When asked about his combat operations, Ramon always politely but firmly declined to speak about that part of his life.

He left the Air Force in 1983 to earn an electrical and computer engineering degree from Tel Aviv University. While at college, he met his future wife Rona at a party, and they were married after a six-month courtship. Upon graduation, Ramon returned to the Air Force and worked his way up the ranks. Then, in 1997, he got a phone call asking if he wanted to apply to become an astronaut. "I thought it was a joke," Ramon recalled, because in Israel the word "astronaut" is often used as an insult to describe someone who's unstable or has his head in the clouds.

It wasn't — and Ramon was soon chosen as his homeland's first astronaut. "When I was a kid, nobody in Israel ever dreamed of being an astronaut because it wasn't on the agenda," Ramon said. "So I never thought I would be an astronaut. When I was selected to be an astronaut, I jumped almost to space. I was very excited."

Ramon and his wife, Rona, moved to Houston in 1998 so he could begin training. Last summer, the couple sent their four children to a camp in Bruceville, Texas, operated by the Union of American Hebrew Congregations. During a visit, Ramon was greeted by about two dozen Israeli staffers clutching metal bicycle helmets that looked like space helmets, recalled camp director Loui Dobin. "He said to them in Hebrew, 'You guys are future members of the astronaut corps. Now drop and give me 20.'"

Ramon was always amazed at how much attention he received, both from his own country and the world at large. "When I started this, I didn't realize how big it was for Israelis and Jews," he said. "People can't believe it. It's very emotional for me also."

After the tragedy, Ramon's 79-year-old father Eliezer Wolferman, who had actually been reading one of his son's emails from space on Israeli TV when he learned of Columbia's destruction, said, "I think of everything from the day he was born until now. I have no son. It is very sad." Ramon's older brother Gadi said, "We are in shock. Everything was working by the book until now. Before this happened we were in a state of euphoria because this was the dream of Ilan." And Isracli Prime Minister Ariel Sharon said, "The state of Israel and its citizens are as one at this difficult time."

For the Israeli people, Ramon brought light to their nation. As the shuttle passed over Israel during Columbia's flight, the war hero sent a message to his nation: "From space, Israel appeared small and very beautiful. The quiet that envelops space makes the beauty even more powerful, and I only hope that the quiet can one day spread to my country."

Chapter 4
The Mission

For a while, it looked as though STS-107 might never make it into space. First scheduled to fly in July 2001, the star-crossed Columbia mission was plagued by a series of setbacks that repeatedly delayed the launch date.

When the science and command crews were announced in late 2000, Columbia was still undergoing renovation at Rockwell International's shuttle facility in Palmdale, California. Unfortunately, the work took longer than expected, and Columbia didn't make it back to Kennedy Space Center until early 2002. Delays continued to accumulate because of setbacks with preceding missions, mechanical problems and a change in mission flight sequence demanded by the need to keep the International Space Station supplied and to rotate the crew.

Finally, STS-107 was reassigned to fly in July 2002, and by late June Columbia had been prepared for launch and waited in the Orbiter Processing Facility at Kennedy Space Center for transfer to the giant Vehicle Assembly Building to be mated with the external fuel tank and solid rocket boosters.

At the last minute, word came from the shuttle management team to put all work on hold. An alert technician had found small cracks in metal liners inside the 12-inch-wide liquid hydrogen fuel lines leading to main engine Number 1 of Columbia's sister ship Discovery during an inspection. Could the same thing have happened to Columbia's plumbing? No one knew, but NASA wasn't about to launch a shuttle with a possible fuel line problem.

Ron Dittemore, Space Shuttle Program Manager, explained the importance of investigating the problem before proceeding:

"These cracks may pose a safety concern and we have teams at work investigating all aspects of the situation. This is a very complex issue and it is early in the analysis. Right now there are more questions than answers. Our immediate interests are to inspect the hardware to identify cracks that exist, understand what has caused them and quantify the risk. I am confident the team will fully resolve this issue, but it may take some time. Until we have a better understanding, we will not move forward with the launch of STS-107."

When similar cracks were found in Atlantis' fuel system, the entire fleet was grounded, with no date set for resumption of shuttle flights. What's more, the fix required the removal of the main engines, further extending the delay. But despite all the problems, the crew remained in good spirits. "We have had a fair number of slips through the course of our training, but we've made good use of those," said mission commander Rick Husband after learning of the new delay. "This will be no different."

In fact, the crew used the downtime in a unique way: they embarked on a wilderness training course. One of NASA's chief concerns about long-duration space flight had always been the personality factor. Could putting a crew of people from different racial, ethnic and philosophical backgrounds in close quarters for weeks at a time cause friction among them and hamper their mission? To find out, the agency tapped the National Outdoor Leadership School, based in Lander, Wyoming, to lead a program that would build leadership and cooperation in the astronaut corps on 12-day expeditions through some of the most rugged backcountry in America. The STS-107 group was the first space shuttle crew to take the course.

At first glance, the Columbia crew might

seem to be especially at risk of developing interpersonal problems. Not only did the group include an Indian, an African-American and an Israeli, but their religious roots were different as well - the crew included a Unitarian, a Jew and at least three Christians. On top of that, two of the crew had been test pilots, a demographic not known for its subtlety.

Nevertheless, the group came together as an especially close-knit team during their trek. Led by guide John Kanengieter, the crew separated into two groups and traveled 35 miles across the rocky, heavily forested Wind River Mountains. They were led by a guide for the first few days, then left on their own to find their way to distant Wind River Peak with only their maps and compasses to guide them. Each day, a different crewmember would lead the group, giving everyone a taste of command — and extra responsibility.

After several days of hiking, the two groups met at the base of the peak. To climb it or not was their choice, but the reunited crew decided it would be a challenge they would tackle together. The climb to the 13,192-foot summit was arduous, but after several hours they all made it to the top and were greeted by a breathtaking view, inspiring Husband to break out in a rousing rendition of "Amazing Grace." After some surprised looks, he was joined in song by the rest of the crew.

Meanwhile, back at the Kennedy Space Center, the fuel-line investigation continued. By then, 11 cracks had been found: Three in Columbia's engines, three on both Atlantis and Discovery and two on Endeavor. When engineers even found cracks in a test engine at the Stennis Space Center in Mississippi, which hadn't been fired in years, they concluded that the shuttle fleet had been flying with cracked fuel lines for some time.

After extensive review, NASA settled on a fix for the cracked pipes: a combination welding/polishing technique that would prevent pieces of the tubing from breaking loose during launch. Columbia's flight was then rescheduled for no earlier than November 29, 2002.

As workers began the painstaking process of repairing the engine flow lines on Atlantis, due to be the next shuttle launched, they discovered yet another problem: cracks in the engine's bearings. As if that wasn't bad enough, it was also discovered that bearings in the giant crawler/transporter that brings the shuttle stack to the launch pad also had cracked bearings, requiring replacement of dozens of the custom-made, volleyball-sized spheres.

As repairs to the crawler began, the shuttle launch team reviewed the bearing data, ran computer simulations and conducted stress tests on similar bearings to determine if Columbia's would need replacing. Because the work could not be done at the launch pad, the ship would have to be rolled back to the Vehicle Assembly Building for repair, further delaying a mission that was already two years behind. In addition, more delays would put the mission in conflict with other launches from the Cape. Eventually, mission planners determined that the bearings would hold and cleared Columbia for launch. On Sunday, January 12, the countdown clock began to tick toward a liftoff the following Thursday.

Ever since the attack on the World Trade Center on September 11, 2001, security at the Cape had been extra-tight before a launch. But the addition of Israeli astronaut Ilan Ramon made the shuttle a tempting target, and NASA began the process of beefing up those already extensive security measures.

On January 14, crews began to load liquid hydrogen and oxygen into Columbia's tanks to power the fuel cells that provide electricity to the spaceship while in orbit. Others loaded food into lockers on the ship's mid-deck, while the experiments that would be conducted were stowed in the Spacehab module in the cargo bay.

Spacehab had flown on 17 previous shuttle missions, but this was the first flight of the new Research Double Module (RDM), designed especially for scientific experimentation. The Spacehab Corporation was founded in 1984 to develop laboratory and habitat modules for the space shuttle, since the orbiter's cramped crew quarters didn't provide nearly enough room for research. A Spacehab single module was first flown in 1993, with a double module being launched three years later. The RDM was designed to improve on the earlier versions, providing more power for experiments, better environmental controls and communication capabilities, and more storage room. NASA leases the modules from Spacehab, which is responsible for their maintenance and inspection. On STS-107, NASA paid $47.65 million for use of the module.

The Spacehab Research Double Module is connected to the shuttle with a pressurized tunnel that allows easy access to the laboratory through the orbiter's mid-deck area. The cylindrical module is 18.4 feet long and 13.5 feet in diameter, large enough to quadruple the living and working area aboard the shuttle. It can hold up to 9,000 pounds of research equipment and adds 2,200 cubic feet of useful space.

On STS-107 the RDM was home to 86 payloads and 79 science experiments, most of which had to be loaded at the launch pad. Because the shuttle, and hence the Spacehab module, sits in a vertical position on the pad, workers had to be repeatedly lowered from the shuttle's mid-deck through the tunnel and into the RDM, carrying the experiments and other items needed for the mission. The entire process took about 20 hours.

Columbia's mission was to conduct a series of scientific tests and experiments that could not yet be done on the International Space Station in its unfinished state. The flight manifest reflected the mission's life sciences objectives and included bees, ants, fish eggs, spiders, silkworms and cocoons, a few fish and 13 rats. Many of the experiments were designed by students and were created to learn how the weightless state in microgravity acts upon animals and insects.

Finally, after two years of preparation and setbacks, both the vehicle and crew were ready to fly. As the crewmembers tried to get in a final few hours of sleep before the launch, Columbia sat majestically on pad 39-A, glowing a brilliant white in the glare of searchlights. In less than 24 hours she would be in space.

※ ※ ※

Thursday 1/16/03

At 2 a.m. Eastern Standard Time, mission managers give the launch team a "go" to begin filling the big external tank with liquid hydrogen and liquid oxygen.

3:06 a.m. Fueling begins, and thousands of gallons of super-cooled rocket fuel flow from spherical storage tanks at the pad through large pipes into the two receptacles inside the external tank. 143,000 gallons of liquid oxygen chilled to -298 degrees F. fill the upper tank, while 385,000 gallons of liquid hydrogen at a temperature of -423 degrees F. flow into the lower tank. At 5:48 a.m. the tanking procedure is complete.

5:52 a.m. The Final Inspection Team arrives at the pad to carefully examine the entire launch vehicle for any last-minute problems. Just as a pilot inspects his plane before flight, the team checks every inch of the external tank, solid rocket boosters and orbiter for any signs of trouble. They are especially on the lookout for ice buildup on the shuttle and external tank, since a chunk of ice shaken loose during the heat and vibration of launch could seriously damage the shuttle. The six-member team also checks the pad for loose objects that could pose a danger to the craft, and makes sure the foam insulation covering the external tank is undamaged and ready for flight. Their tools include an infrared scanner that can simply be pointed at an object to determine its temperature, enabling it to spot areas where the frigid rocket fuel might be leaking, or even worse, burning. Each crewmember wears a heat-resistant jumpsuit designed to prevent static buildup, since even a brief arc of static electricity could be deadly near the ultra-flammable fuel. Also taking up their posts are members of the Closeout Crew, who have the job of getting the orbiter's cabin ready for the astronauts.

7:30 a.m. At the Operations and Checkout Building, the crew of Columbia boards the van that will take them to Launch Complex 39-A. They arrive at the pad a few minutes later and take the elevator up to the 195-foot level where the Closeout Crew waits to help them into the orbiter.

7:52 a.m. The astronauts begin entering the shuttle, taking their positions in the cabin while the Closeout Crew helps them strap in. Commander Rick Husband goes first, taking the front left seat on the flight deck. Payload Specialist Ilan Ramon is next. He takes the rightmost seat on the mid-deck, just below the flight deck. Pilot Willie McCool follows, sitting beside Husband on the flight deck. Payload Commander Michael Anderson boards the shuttle next, taking the left seat on the mid-deck. Mission Specialist David Brown makes his way to his assigned seat behind McCool, then Mission Specialist Laurel Clark enters Columbia and sits in the center seat on the mid-deck. Last aboard is Mission Specialist and Flight Engineer Kalpana Chawla, who sits on the flight deck in the center seat.

9:11 a.m. With all the astronauts aboard and settled in, the Closeout Crew is instructed to close Columbia's hatch and perform pressure tests and leak checks to make sure it's secure.

9:51 a.m. Husband begins to pressurize the Orbital Maneuvering System's fuel, used to guide the craft while in orbit, while McCool does the same for the Auxiliary Power Units that supply electricity to the spacecraft. Meanwhile, the launch computers arm the charges that are used to separate the spacecraft from its hold-down posts and various other connection points at ignition.

10:16 a.m. Mission Control in Houston loads the spacecraft's computers with the critical guidance data that will be needed to put Columbia into its designated orbit.

10:27 a.m. A final poll of all spacecraft systems is taken by Test Director Jeff Spaulding. One by one, each launch team member reports that his part of the system is ready for launch. Mission Control reports no problems with the weather either at Kennedy Space Center or at the possible abort sites overseas. Columbia is Go for launch.

10:30 a.m. A computer called the Ground Launch Sequencer takes over the last few minutes of the countdown at T-minus 9 minutes and counting. The computer is able to constantly check a thousand parameters to make sure they're in bounds, something no human could possibly do.

10:31 a.m. The computer begins to move the steel access arm the astronauts used to board Columbia away from the vehicle. It is T-minus 7 minutes 30 seconds.

10:33 a.m. The orbiter's Auxiliary Power Units are pre-started and ready for activation at T-minus 5 minutes 30 seconds. The APUs provide electric and hydraulic power for the spacecraft.

10:34 a.m. McCool starts up Columbia's three APUs. Outside the ship fighter jets maintain a wide perimeter around the launch pad, while radar scans for intruders, but everything still looks good for launch.

10:35 a.m. The three main engines are gimbaled, or moved through a pre-arranged pattern, to make sure they're ready for flight. They will help steer Columbia toward orbit during descent.

10:36 a.m. The vent hood atop the external tank, which allows gaseous oxygen to escape so as not to overpressurize the tank, is moved aside. At Mission Control, Launch Director Mike Leinbach tells the astronauts to close and lock their helmet visors. "If there ever was a time to use the phrase 'all good things come to people

The crew of STS-107 heads for the Columbia launch pad on January 16, 2003

A close-up camera view shows space shuttle Columbia as it lifts off from Launch Pad 39A at Kennedy Space Center

Spewing flames and billowing clouds of smoke, Columbia roars toward space. Crowds in the VIP stands, including friends and relatives of the seven astronauts, cheer Columbia as it rises from the launch pad

Astronaut David M. Brown (bottom) exercises on the bicycle ergometer as Israeli Ilan Ramon (top) types on a laptop computer on the flight deck of Columbia

Columbia crew members pose for a photo in the SPACEHAB research double module

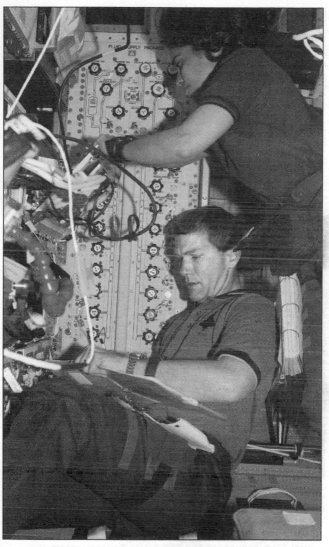

Commander Rick Husband (sitting) and Mission Specialist Kalpana Chawla share experiment-monitoring chores

Above, debris from Columbia streaks across the sky over Tyler, Texas on the morning of Saturday, February 1, 2003. At right, top, contrails from the space shuttle flash across the sky over Texas. Right center, after Mission Control lost touch with Columbia, pieces of the space shuttle rained from the sky. Right bottom, a shooting star – the last images the world would have of Columbia

David Brown (from left to right), Ilan Ramon, Rick Husband, Kalpana Chawla, William McCool, Michael Anderson and Laurel Clark talk about the Teacher In Space program as an apple floats in the zero-gravity foreground

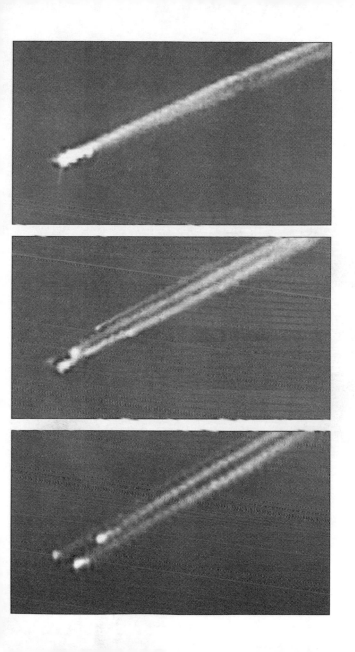

NASA Administrators Sean O'Keefe (left) and William Readdy, (right), a former shuttle commander, try to fight off emotion as they speak at a press conference about the seven lost astronauts

Milt Heflin, NASA's chief flight director, pauses at a press conference covering the tragic loss of Columbia

Mac Powell examines a large piece of Columbia that dropped onto his Texas ranch

4:50PM
FEB 1 2003

A helmet that fell into a yard in Norwood Community, Texas, from the space shuttle Columbia

An official from NASA stares at a piece of the space shuttle that landed in a front yard

Wink Miller looks at a piece of debris he found in the trees near Hemphill, Texas

Tommy Peltier (above, with his daughter Alexis) points in the direction he witnessed this huge piece of debris fall from. At right, a charred backpack was among body parts and debris that scattered over many states

MISSION COMMANDER COLONEL RICK HUSBAND

At left, Husband shares his enthusiasm for space travel with students at Bushland Independent School

At left, sitting in the cockpit of Columbia, Husband participates in a simulated launch countdown a month before liftoff. Top, he arrives at Kennedy Space Center, eager to take part in Terminal Countdown Demonstration Test activities. At right, Husband suits up for STS-107

PILOT WILLIAM "WILLIE" MCCOOL

Happy to be suiting up, Columbia pilot William "Willie" McCool is ready for launch

Ready for anything — McCool takes an emergency training session in stride

Columbia pilot William McCool stands before a T-38 jet he flew before taking the controls of Columbia

Anderson prepares a high-tech exercise bike for tests that will monitor human respiratory functions in space

Anderson floats over Israeli astronaut Ilan Ramon (right) while David Brown is in the background of Columbia's SPACEHAB

PAYLOAD COMMANDER MICHAEL ANDERSON

STS-107 Payload Commander Michael Anderson is ready for countdown on the morning of the launch

MISSION SPECIALIST KALPANA CHAWLA

Mission Specialist Kalpana Chawla poses for pictures a month before her second trip into space

Above, Chawla is pictured on the flight deck of Columbia during the crew's first full day in space. At right, she poses with her husband for preflight publicity photos

Mission Specialist David Brown poses for a photo upon arrival to Kennedy Space Center

He poses with neighbor Jill Swindell shortly before Columbia lifted off on its date with destiny

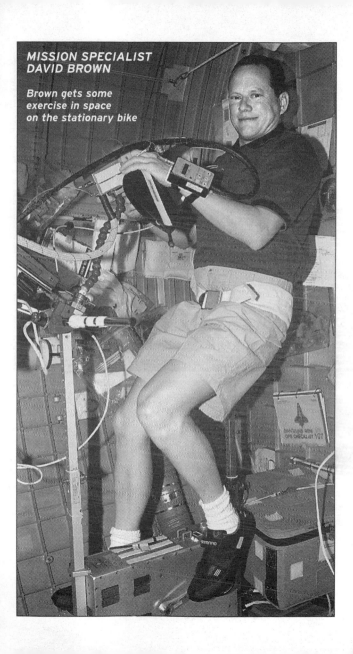

MISSION SPECIALIST
DAVID BROWN

Brown gets some
exercise in space
on the stationary bike

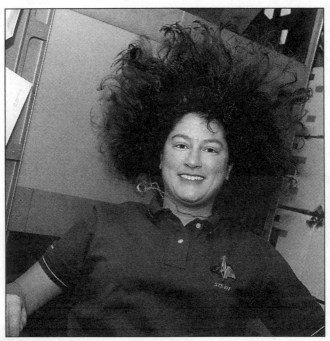

MISSION SPECIALIST LAUREL CLARK

Above, letting her hair out – astronaut Laurel Clark floats in zero-gravity space. At left, all smiles – she arrives at Kennedy Space Center to take part in preflight testing procedures

She gets a final fitting on her suit just two days before Columbia would blast into space

PAYLOAD SPECIALIST ILAN RAMON

Ilan Ramon, posing for a photo upon arrival to Kennedy Space Center, was a payload specialist on STS-107

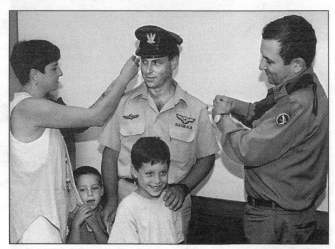

Ilan Ramon (center), here photographed with the wife and children he left behind. He is receiving his colonel rank epaulettes from Israeli Chief of General Staff Ehud Barak (right)

The former Israeli war hero was the first Israeli astronaut

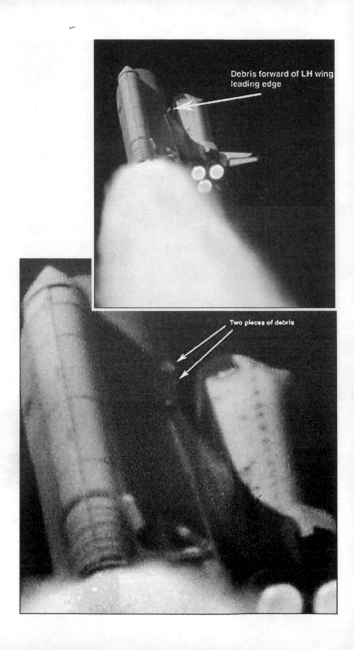

Debris forward of LH wing leading edge

Two pieces of debris

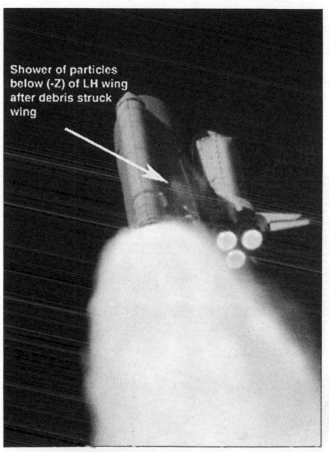

Shower of particles below (-Z) of LH wing after debris struck wing

Top left, only seconds after liftoff, cameras capture a piece of debris hitting the left wing of Columbia. At left, breaking off from the external tanks, two pieces of debris hit the shuttle after liftoff. Above, more debris breaks from the solid rocket booster to hit Columbia. The possibility that heat-resistant tiles may have been dislodged, dooming the space shuttle from the start, became the early focus of investigators

Don Maxwell coordinates the broad search for Columbia debris, fully aware that many pieces of the doomed Columbia might not be found for years to come

Workers examine a piece of the space shuttle as they prepare to reconstruct the orbiter for the exhaustive investigation ahead

A truckload of recovered debris from Columbia arrives at a hanger near the Shuttle Landing Facility

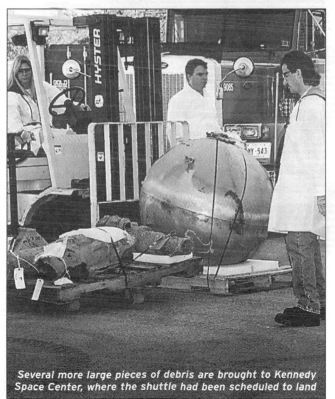

Several more large pieces of debris are brought to Kennedy Space Center, where the shuttle had been scheduled to land

Above: William McCool (left) and Rick Husband (right). At left: Michael Anderson (left) and Ilan Ramon (right). Below: Husband (left) and McCool (right). Opposite page: Bottom left: Kalpana Chawla (left) and Laurel Clark (right). Bottom right: Chawla (left) and Ramon (right)

Guides Andy Cline and John Kanengieter (from left to right)
help astronauts Laurel Clark, Rick Husband and Ilan Ramon
with a map during a training hike designed to test
interpersonal skills. Despite different backgrounds,
the Columbia crew would work seamlessly together

NASA T-38 jets fly over a memorial service in the "missing man" formation to honor the seven lost astronauts

Somber faces fill a memorial service for the crew of Columbia held at Kennedy Space Center on February 7, 2003

who wait,' this is it," adds Leinbach. "From the many, many people who put this mission together, good luck and godspeed."

10:38 a.m. At T-minus 31 seconds, Columbia's onboard computers take over the launch sequence. At T-minus 16 seconds, thousands of gallons of water begin to flood the pad to suppress the sound and vibration of launch. At T-minus 10 seconds, igniters near the main engine nozzles fire to burn off any excess hydrogen that may have accumulated. At T-minus 6.6 seconds, the main engines roar to life.

10:39 a.m. As a plume of flame appears below the main engines, the solid rocket boosters flare to life. The ground shakes for miles around as Columbia slowly rises on a wide apron of fire, gaining speed. At T+20 seconds, the computers have rolled the ship to a heading that will take it into the proper orbit. The engines briefly throttle back to 67 percent of their rated performance level as the shuttle passes through the point of maximum aerodynamic pressure, then throttle up to 104 percent power at T+60 seconds.

10:40 a.m. Just 90 seconds after liftoff, the shuttle has burned so much fuel it weighs just half what it did on the pad.

10:41 a.m. Their fuel expended, the two solid rocket boosters separate at two minutes ten seconds into the flight. They will descend on parachutes and be recovered for a future flight.

10:43 a.m. Columbia reaches the point where a return to the Kennedy Space Center is no longer possible in the event of a problem.

10:47 a.m. The shuttle's main engines have done their job and shut off just 8 minutes and 30 seconds after liftoff. After two long years, the crew is finally in orbit. The external tank separates from the orbiter's belly and begins its long fall back toward Earth, where it will burn up on re-entry.

Still ahead are several more tasks, including several firings of the OMS engines to put Columbia into its final orbital position, and the opening of the 60-foot long cargo bay doors. But for now the crew celebrates, elated to be in space at last.

After congratulations all around, it's time to get to work. This mission promises to be a grueling one for the astronauts, requiring 12-hour days packed with constant activity. To keep the experiments and other tasks going 24 hours a day, the crew is split into two teams to share the duties. Husband, Chawla, Clark and Ramon will be on the Red Team, while McCool, Brown and Anderson will comprise the Blue Team. The crew immediately begins to unload the stowed items in the shuttle mid-deck, then check out and activate Spacehab. At 3:47 p.m., it's bedtime for the Blue

Team, but they'll be up just six hours later so the Red Team can get some shuteye.

* * *

Friday 1/17 /03

The Israeli Mediterranean Dust Experiment, or MEIDEX, is checked and activated. The MEIDEX experiment, developed at Tel Aviv University, is designed to study the transport of mineral dust in the atmosphere over the Mediterranean Sea and the tropical Atlantic Ocean. One purpose of MEIDEX is to determine the role that aerosols, especially desert dust, play in weather and climate conditions in many parts of the world and the Middle East in particular. During STS-107 MEIDEX was used to study effects of desert dust and smoke plumes on the climate and obtained important still images and video to be studied in the future. The MEIDEX experiment also resulted in the first calibrated images of an atmospheric phenomenon known as an "elf," an elusive electrical halo that glows over the tops of some thunderstorms.

The crew broadcasts close-ups of their ant colony, composed of fifteen harvester ants busy building tunnels in a glass enclosure filled with a transparent gel. The experiment, designed by a science class from Fowler High School in Syracuse, New York, determined that ants move faster in space than they do on Earth.

Another experiment, Mechanics of Granular Materials, was created to improve the understanding of how earthquakes damage soil and building foundations. When an earthquake strikes, it can cause soil to act more like a liquid, but the exact process isn't well understood. Because the process can't be well-duplicated on Earth, MGM is making its third flight on a shuttle.

Saturday 1/18/03

MEIDEX is once again used to study Mediterranean dust, while an experiment that looks at the movement of calcium through the body begins. To help scientists understand the phenomenon of bone loss in space, some of the crew swallows calcium tracers that will be monitored to see how calcium is metabolized by the body during spaceflight.

Red Team members take a few minutes away from their experiments to talk with reporters from CNN, CBS News and Fox News Channel.

Sunday 1/19/03

Ilan Ramon begins experiments in Spacehab's complex combustion module, an enclosed chamber in which fires can be lit without endangering the rest of the spacecraft. In Earth's gravity, flame and combustion studies are affected by turbulence, but in zero gravity, flames are symmetrical and even. That allows a much more precise look at how a flame creates soot, a major pollutant on Earth. The data gained is to be provided to U.S. aircraft engine manufacturers to help them refine engine combustion processes, reducing soot emissions. Ramon reports that the combustion module works perfectly.

The MGM experiment is operated again, and a series of biomedical experiments are begun to examine how the body manufactures protein in a zero-g environment, as well as how bone and calcium is produced and how saliva and urine change in space.

* * *

Monday 1/20/03

The combustion module is put to use again, and the biomedical studies continue. Crew members take turns drawing each other's blood to study how their bodies are adapting to weightlessness. The MGM experiment captures images of a "sprite," an electrical phenomenon similar to an elf in that it sometimes appears above large thunderstorms, but which is associated with discharges from storm clouds into Earth's upper atmosphere. Mission Specialist Laurel Clark starts up the Microbial Physiology Flight Experiment, which begins to study how fungi react in microgravity.

Controllers note a leak in Spacehab's cooling system, and open a valve that allows cool air to flow into the module from Columbia. A duct is later extended into Spacehab to divert air from the shuttle into the science module.

＊ ＊ ＊

Tuesday 1/21/03

Ilan Ramon speaks with Israeli Prime Minister Ariel Sharon from orbit. He captures a picture of an elf to add to his previous shot of sprites.

Instruments which study the ozone layer had been mounted in the payload bay. Husband steers the ship to aim these instruments at Earth.

The Bioreactor Demonstration System, a device which can grow biological cultures much better than Earthbound laboratories, begins studying prostate cancer cells. Mission Specialist and medical doctor Laurel Clark monitors the experiment, which may help to unlock the secrets of this deadly disease.

＊ ＊ ＊

Wednesday 1/22/03

It's TV day on Columbia as the crew broadcasts images of some of the experiments: the Fowler High School ants busily tunneling through their gel; one from Glen Waverly Secondary College of Melbourne, Australia showing Garden Orb Weaver spiders trying to build webs in zero-g; a silkworm larvae experiment designed by students at Jingshan School, Beijing, China; carpenter bees boring tunnels for their nests; and a Tokyo Institute of Technology experiment with developing fish embryos.

The Blue Team's work with the SOFBALL (Structures of Flame Balls at Low Lewis-Number) experiment results in the weakest flame ever produced, invisible to the human eye but visible through special optical equipment. Scientists hope the experiment will provide insight into low-power combustion, which could lead to new, more efficient types of internal combustion engines.

✳ ✳ ✳

Thursday 1/23/03

Dave Brown and Ilan Ramon operate the Advanced Respiratory Monitoring System, an experiment from the European Space Agency. ARMS targets the human lung and circulatory system and the human muscular system, watching for changes induced by the zero-g environment.

Laurel Clark continues her experiments with prostate tissue, and sends data from the Advanced Astroculture experiment to Mission Control. Astroculture, sponsored by International Flavors and Fragrances, Inc. of New York, aims to extract essential oils from space-grown flowers for possible use in perfumes.

To acknowledge the Blue Team's work with flame production, Mission Control wakes them up at the end of their scheduled sleep period with a recording of 'Burning Down the House' by Talking Heads.

✳ ✳ ✳

Friday 1/24/03

Columbia is put into "free drift" mode so its thrusters won't affect the SOFBALL experiment. The last of six samples of essential oils from the Astroculture experiment are harvested. Work continues on the MGM soil-compacting experiment.

✳ ✳ ✳

Saturday 1/25/03

Willie McCool, Dave Brown and Michael Anderson take a few minutes to be interviewed by Black Entertainment TV, WTKR-TV in Norfolk, Va., and KNSD-TV in San Diego.

Laurel Clark completes her bone cell experiments and continues work on the Bioreactor Demonstration System, still growing prostate cancer tissues to learn how the cancer spreads within the body and into its bones. She also works on an experiment focusing on how yeast and bacteria develop in space and how weightlessness might affect their antibiotic response.

Ilan Ramon beams down a video showing the progress of various experiments around the shuttle and in Spacehab.

* * *

Sunday 1/26/03

The student experiments bear fruit: A fish hatches in one, and in another a silk moth emerges from its cocoon.

The MEIDEX experiment records significant dust plumes over the Mediterranean and successfully downlinks the data, including both still images and video, to Mission Control. The video contains breathtaking views of the Middle East from orbit.

Mike Anderson and Dave Brown conduct the final combustion chamber experiments, after which they reconfigure the chamber for the

Water Mist Fire Suppression Experiment (MIST), which will study zero-g fire suppression techniques.

* * *

Monday 1/27/03

With many of their experiments completed, Husband, Chawla, Clark and Ramon take some time to chat with the International Space Station crew via a ship-to-ship link. ISS Commander Ken Bowersox, NASA ISS Science Officer Don Pettit and Flight Engineer Nikolai Budarin are delighted at the unusual communication.

The Structures of Flame Balls experiment is wrapped up after a total of 55 flaming spheres have been ignited, including the weakest and leanest flames ever burned. The longest-lived flame burned for 81 minutes.

* * *

Tuesday 1/28/03

MIST has to wait while the crew attempts to fix the leaky combustion chamber. It will be used to develop lighter, more effective fire suppression systems on Earth as well as to investigate better methods of fire control aboard spacecraft.

Clark retrieves samples from the Bioreactor

Demonstration System, and reports growing a prostate cancer tumor tissue sample as large as a golf ball - the largest sample ever grown in space. She also continues the physiology and biochemistry experiment by collecting blood and urine samples from her crewmates.

Chawla reports that the MIST chamber is watertight at last.

* * *

Wednesday 1/29/03

With scientific work winding down, the crewmembers conduct a news conference. Ilan Ramon remarks on how peaceful the world looks from Earth's orbit. "The world looks marvelous from up here, so peaceful, so wonderful and so fragile," he says. "The atmosphere is so thin and fragile, and I think all of us have to keep it clean and good. It saves our life and gives us life."

Michael Anderson is very happy about the success of Columbia's mission, and suggests that even better days are to come. "I think once we get a seven-member crew on board the space station you're really going to see some outstanding science in space," he says. "A lot of experiments that we have are really just being demonstrated and developed. Once they're fully developed they'll reside on board the space station and the scientists will have years to conduct the experiments that we're trying to do here in a relatively short period of time."

The repaired Combustion Module Facility containing the Water Mist Fire Suppression Experiment manages 14 sample runs.

* * *

Thursday 1/30/03

The crew begins to stow blood, urine and saliva samples in refrigeration systems and to wrap up the last of the experiments.

Rick Husband and Kalpana Chawla take turns simulating landing with an onboard computer training system called PILOT.

Forecasts call for ideal weather conditions at the Kennedy Space Center Shuttle Landing Facility at touchdown time.

* * *

Friday 1/31/03

The last of the experiments are deactivated and secured. Chawla, McCool and Husband start up one of Columbia's Auxiliary Power Units and check the operation of the ship's flight control surfaces. Everything appears normal. The crew also successfully test-fires the attitude thrusters that control the shuttle's position both in space and during descent. The Spacehab module is powered down for the return to Earth.

The favorable landing forecast holds, with light winds expected and few, if any, clouds. The crew spends their final night in space.

Chapter 5
Birth of a Spaceship

On April 12, 1981, Commander John Young and Pilot Robert Crippen were strapped inside the Columbia, prepared to take the very first shuttle into space on its maiden voyage. When it took to the sky, the craft was the most sophisticated – and the most complicated – flying machine ever built. With 2.5 million parts, including 230 miles of wire, 1,060 plumbing valves and connections, 1,440 circuit breakers, and more than 27,000 insulating tiles and thermal blankets, this was one of mankind's most magnificent accomplishments.

The seeds of the space shuttle program had been sown decades earlier. In 1947, the popular press had captured the public's collective imagination with A Trip to the Moon and Back, a collection of fanciful stories speculating what it might be like to travel to the moon in a rocket.

Later, in 1954, Collier's magazine published a series of futuristic articles written by the German rocket scientist Wernher von Braun, who described large cargo-carrying rocket ships that would not only ferry astronauts and materials between Earth and orbit, but would be able to return to space again and again, requiring a much smaller investment than the expendable rockets that existed at the time.

By the late '50s, with America's space race against the Russians gearing up to full speed, the development of reusable spacecraft was put on the back burner so that the Saturn V could be developed. The Russians had been first to orbit a spacecraft — the tiny Sputnik — and at the time it looked as though they might be first to set foot on the moon as well. In a 1961 memo, President Kennedy asked Vice President Lyndon Johnson if there was a program that would help the nation restore its prominence in space:

Do we have a chance of beating the Soviets by putting a laboratory in space, or by a trip around the moon, or by a rocket to land on the moon, or by a rocket to go to the moon and back with a man? Is there any other space program which promises dramatic results in which we could win?

Johnson replied that a moon landing was possible by the end of the decade, and stressed that any nation to accomplish it would be regarded as a world leader. With nothing less than national pride at stake, Kennedy gave the famous speech at Rice University on September 12, 1962 in which he dedicated America's collective efforts to the moon race.

As the Mercury, Gemini and Apollo programs continued through the 1960s, engineers still puzzled over the possibilities of reusable spacecraft. It was obvious that an expensive behemoth like the Saturn, which dumped most of its stages into the ocean in order to get the small Apollo capsule into orbit, was impractical for regular access to space. By February 1967, with the moon landing still two years away, the President's Science Advisory Committee noted the need for a space transportation system: "For the longer range, studies should be made of more economical ferrying systems, presumably involving partial or total recovery and use." Thus, the concept of a two-part system began to take shape: a large detachable booster which could be recovered and returned to base, and a cargo-carrying component which would be able to return from space and land on a conventional runway.

On January 5, 1972, President Richard Nixon set the shuttle program in motion. "The United States should proceed at once with the development of an entirely new type of space transportation system designed to help transform the space frontier of the 1970s into familiar territory, easily accessible for human endeavor, in the 1980s and '90s," he said. "It will revolutionize transportation into near space by routinizing it . . . It will take the astronomical costs out of astronautics . . . This is why commitment to the space shuttle's program is the right next step for America to take."

NASA's first shuttle design was fully reusable, with both the booster and orbiter being manned and capable of returning to their launch site. The orbiter would sit piggyback on the booster and be launched vertically just as all rockets had been up until that time. Both would be powered by liquid hydrogen and oxygen carried in internal tanks. The booster would carry the orbiter skyward until nearly in space, then separate and descend to a landing while the orbiter continued its climb. Designers emphasized that because neither vessel dropped fuel tanks, this system was considerably safer than those designed around expendable boosters.

The problem with the design, however, was its expense. Even though it was desirable to have a completely reusable system, NASA recognized that Congress would never approve such a costly program, and went back to the drawing board. What emerged in 1971 was the concept of a partly reusable system, with a large fuel tank that would be discarded after it was empty, two solid fuel boosters that would be retrieved and reused, and an orbiter that would return to a runway at mission's end.

In July 1972, following intense competition among the major aerospace manufacturers, NASA awarded North American Rockwell Corporation the contract to build the orbiter. The final design was 122 feet long, with a 78-foot wingspan, and a cargo bay that was 60 feet long and 15 feet wide — large enough to carry multiple satellites into orbit. The orbiter would be mounted on a 154-foot-long external fuel tank that contained two internal tanks which held liquid hydrogen and oxygen rocket fuel. When both tanks were filled before launch, the monster would weigh a staggering 1.7 million pounds.

Martin Marietta Corporation was selected to build the tank, while the Morton Thiokol Corporation was selected to build the two solid rocket boosters (SRBs) which would provide the extra boost needed to get the giant stack of hardware into orbit. Measuring 149 feet long and capable of contributing more than three million pounds of thrust each, the SRBs were impressive in their own right.

With the general design of the ship settled and all major contractors on board, teams of engineers set to work on the details. Whereas the Saturn V's motors were designed for only a single use, the shuttle needed an entirely new type of liquid-fuel rocket engine. It would need more sophisticated propulsion that provided variable thrust, and it would have to be tough enough to propel the spacecraft into orbit again and again. In 1972, Rockwell's Rocketdyne Division began to create what would become the world's most sophisticated rocket engine ever.

What emerged on the engine designers' drawing boards was a relatively small power plant with amazing thrust capacity. The final design of the Space Shuttle Main Engine (SSME) was 14 feet tall and 8 feet wide and weighed around 7,000 pounds — very light for a rocket engine. The liquid-fueled motors would operate at extremely high internal pressure, around 7,500 pounds per square inch. In comparison, the Atlas rocket that propelled John Glenn into orbit in his Mercury capsule was powered by an engine that developed 900 PSI, and even the giant Saturn V first stage motor developed only 2,000 PSI.

Around 55 percent of the power needed for Columbia to reach orbit would be provided by three SSMEs (Space Shuttle Main Engines), with the remainder of the power coming from the solid rocket boosters. Engineers built in a high degree of redundancy to make the engine as safe as possible, and designed all of its components to be easily replaceable so as to lower the cost per mission. They also made each part as strong as technologically possible, since it was planned that each engine would be used at least fifty times before it needed a major overhaul.

Each main engine was driven by a high-pressure turbo pump and contained more than 3,000 weld points to reduce weight and minimize possible leak paths. The pump was the core of the system, able to build up tremendous power compared to its weight. A car engine is capable of generating about half a horsepower per pound of engine weight, but each of the shuttle's turbopumps builds up 100 horsepower per pound — about 77,000 horsepower for each pump. That's enough pressure to shoot a column of liquid hydrogen 36 miles into the air.

The engines are fed from a giant external tank by a series of pipes capable of moving 3.5 million pounds of propellants through the turbopumps in just eight and a half minutes. In that short time, the three main engines generate 23 times the power produced by the Hoover Dam. If you put all three of the shuttle's engines to work draining an average-sized swimming pool, it could get the job done in less than 25 seconds. The temperature inside the shuttle's main engines reaches more than 6,000 degrees F. during launch, which is higher than the boiling point of iron. That's even more amazing when you consider that the main engine's fuel, liquid hydrogen, is the second coldest liquid on Earth at -423 degrees F.

As might be expected, all this capability didn't come easy. The ambitious and complex nature of the engine design soon gave rise to technological problems. The first prototype engine was completed in March 1975 and a program of test firings began soon afterward. Delays resulted when engine nozzles failed testing procedures and it was found that cracks were beginning to develop in the engine's turbine blades as a result of the hellish temperatures and pressures they were subjected to during use.

As the engine program fell further behind, Washington began to notice. In December 1977, the Senate Subcommittee on Science, Technology, and Space of the Committee on Commerce, Science and Transportation asked the National Research Council to conduct an independent review of the engine development process. The Council's findings indicated that the test program was experiencing the same types of problems inherent in any highly technical development program and issued a few suggestions, among them to delay the first flight.

When an engine was destroyed by fire during testing on December 27, 1978, it began to look as though Columbia would never leave the ground. The National Research Council issued a statement saying the targeted 1980 date for the first flight was unlikely to be met. More ominously, another major problem had reared its head — the shuttle's protective thermal tiles were not working as expected. In fact, the tiles had been a problem from the early stages of the vehicle's design. During the Mercury, Gemini and Apollo programs, spacecraft re-entering the Earth's atmosphere relied on a coating of material designed to protect the craft by slowly burning away. The so-called ablative materials had worked well and given the space program a perfect recovery record for all returning capsules. But those ships were designed for one trip only, and most now reside in museums around the country, their heat shields still attached.

The shuttle, however, was to make repeated trips to and from space and replacing the entire underside of the craft on each flight was simply impractical. After extensive testing, NASA settled on foamed silica (sand) coated with borosilicate glass. This lightweight ceramic material had been developed by Lockheed chemist Robert Beasley, who joined Lockheed Missiles and Space Company in the early 1960s. Lockheed decided Beasley's invention had no practical use and shelved it, saying there was no market for lightweight ceramics. But when the need arose for a relatively inexpensive, heat-insulating substance for the orbiter, Beasley's project was revived. After winning the contract, Lockheed paid him a $90,000 bonus for his invention and set to work creating the thousands of heat-resistant tiles that would cover Columbia's underside.

The tiles were a true breakthrough in space science. They weighed only nine pounds per cubic foot and yet were able to protect the shuttle from temperatures of up to 3,000 degrees F. on re-entry. The material dissipates surface heat so quickly that an uncoated tile can be removed from an oven and held by its edges with a bare hand while its interior still glows red-hot.

But as fantastic as the tiles were, they were also highly problematic. To start with, foamed silica is a very brittle, nonflexible substance, while the Columbia's aluminum frame was designed to stretch and contract slightly depending on temperature and aerodynamic loads. In order to attach the tiles to the spaceship, each tile had to be made specifically for its location on the orbiter and was therefore slightly different in size and shape from its neighbor. Simply keeping track of the tiles, each with its own number and documentation, created mountains of paperwork. Moreover, it would take more than 27,000 tiles to protect Columbia from the fiery heat of re-entry, making the bonding process difficult and intensely time-consuming.

When it became clear that it wouldn't be possible to simply glue the tiles onto the shuttle's aluminum frame, designers proposed that a blanket of Nomex felt be installed between the frame and tiles. The felt would act as an insulator and buffer, and allow the shuttle's frame to flex without popping the tiles off. In 1979, the tiles underwent preliminary testing, and it was discovered that they did not adhere as strongly to the frame as was necessary. Columbia was ferried from California to the Kennedy Space Center in Florida, where work on the thermal protection system continued.

At huge cost, NASA began to "pull-test" the tiles, and any that failed were replaced. By early 1980, ten thousand of the trouble-plagued tiles still remained to be bonded to the orbiter. Costs continued to rise as the project fell further and further behind schedule, despite the efforts of workers who toiled six days a week for 24 hours a day to install the tiles. Budgetary woes were compounded by the vehicle's nose and the leading edges of its wings: they would become much hotter than the rest of the ship and had to be covered with an expensive carbon-carbon material.

As engineers learned more about the actual temperatures the tiles would encounter on the ship's return from orbit, they became increasingly worried that if even a single tile were lost in a critical area it might start a "zipper" effect and result in the loss of the vehicle and crew. With this in mind, they began to explore how the underside of the shuttle might be examined for missing tiles while still in orbit, and developed a tile repair kit for that scenario. The Manned Maneuvering Unit (MMU) was developed to make underbelly repairs, but in a series of simulations it was found that the unit would exhaust its nitrogen gas propellant within five minutes — and even the simplest repair took longer than that. Furthermore, although a repair kit was carried aboard STS-2, it was later abandoned because the sealant didn't adhere properly to the shuttle's liner. When NASA determined that the risk of sending a crew member to complete the almost-impossible task was far greater than the risk posed by missing tiles, efforts to establish tile-repair capability were terminated.

While the tiles required the development of completely new technologies and processes, the same wasn't true for the shuttle's other components. The solid rocket boosters, for example, were refined versions of rockets invented by the Chinese centuries before. While liquid rocket fuel is volatile and must be kept at temperatures below freezing, solid rocket fuel is stable at room temperature and is much more easily handled and stored.

The shuttle's solid boosters are the largest

ever flown and were the first to be used with a manned spacecraft. At 150 feet tall and 12 feet wide, they are strapped to either side of the external tank and provide the extra kick needed to obtain orbital speed. Solid-fuel boosters were chosen for several reasons: they're more reliable than liquid-fueled rockets, lighter in weight and simpler in design. Because they were intended to sink to the bottom of the ocean after separation from the external tank, the less-complex design was considered a major selling point.

The boosters are made up of several segments bolted together at so-called field joints filled with a heat-resistant putty and rubber O-rings, which are supposed to protect the joints from burning through during ascent. They would later become a critical point of failure on Challenger. They are filled with a propellant that looks and feels like a pencil eraser. The actual fuel is aluminum powder, with aluminum perchlorate powder mixed in as an oxidizer, needed to supply oxygen to keep the fuel burning. Iron oxide is included to speed up the burn rate, and a polymer binder that is also combustible keeps it all together. The long tube of the booster is hollow in the middle, with a small rocket motor mounted at one end. On ignition, this motor fires and ignites the solid fuel in about 0.15 of a second, and the entire booster is up to its full operating pressure and

3,200 degrees F. temperature in half a second.

All this gas and heat flows through the booster's 12-foot nozzles, adding their thrust to that of the three main engines. The nozzles and main engines can both be steered on command from the ship's computers, controlling the direction of thrust to help steer the shuttle into orbit. Unlike the main engines, though, the solid rocket motors cannot be shut off once they're ignited. As one astronaut put it, "when those solids light up, you know you're going somewhere."

Because a runaway space shuttle could wreak untold havoc, explosive charges in both the solid rocket boosters and the external tank were included in construction. If the space plane were ever to go off course and threaten populated areas, it would be possible for the Range Safety Officer at the Kennedy Space Center to destroy the vehicle before it could harm civilians. Called the Command Destruct System in NASA-speak, the charges are designed to split the boosters open along 70% of their length, immediately terminating their thrust. The system has been used only once: to destroy the careening boosters after Challenger exploded in 1986.

✳ ✳ ✳

While work continued on the shuttle's main components, the Kennedy Space Center was undergoing major changes. Launch complexes 39-A and 39-B, last used for the Apollo and Apollo-Soyuz programs in July 1975, were extensively renovated and refitted to accommodate the new vehicle. The Mobile Service Structures which once carried Saturn V rockets to the pad were upgraded to fit the shuttle, and a new Rotating Service Structure (RSS) was built at both complexes so shuttles could be serviced right at the pad. Before launch, the RSS is rotated away from the vehicle to protect it from the blast of the shuttle's engines. Also added was the 15,000-foot long Shuttle Landing Facility, a 30-foot wide runway carved through the central Florida grasslands.

Because the orbiter would be landing at Edwards Air Force Base in California on its first few missions, and just in case weather prevented a landing at the Kennedy Space Center, NASA needed to create a way to get the vehicle back to Florida. That required the construction of a Mate/Demate Device, a giant complex of girders that could place Columbia atop a modified Boeing 747 ferry craft and remove it once it reached its destination.

During the construction of Columbia, designated to be the first space shuttle to reach space, another shuttle was being built — but it would never fly beyond Earth's atmosphere. Orbiter Vehicle 101 was to be a flying testbed to check out the aerodynamic stability of the airframe. OV-101 was originally to be named Constitution in honor of the U.S. Constitution's bicentennial, but fans of the Star Trek television show lobbied to name the ship Enterprise, and in September 1976 a gleaming white shuttle bearing that name emerged from Rockwell International's facility in Palmdale, California. In attendance were many members of the original show's cast.

In the first phase of the program, OV-101 made several flights aboard its 747 carrier to make sure the combination was stable. In the event the shuttle had to be jettisoned, the first few flights were unmanned, but finally, on August 12, 1977, Enterprise separated from its mothership for the first time and flew free. On the flight deck were astronauts Fred W. Haise, Jr. and Charles G. "Gordon" Fullerton. The craft descended from an altitude of 24,000 feet to the Rogers Dry Lakebed desert runway at Edwards Air Force base in just five minutes and 21 seconds, landing successfully at a speed of 213 miles an hour.

By April 1981, Columbia had languished in the Orbiter Processing Facility at Kennedy Space Center for more than 18 months. Plagued with problems with its main engines and Thermal Protection System, the first launch was two years behind schedule and the shuttle program was more than $3.6 billion over budget. Both Congress and the American people were becoming impatient with the slow progress of the mission, which is perhaps why NASA decided to move Columbia to the launch pad on a chilly January day, fully three months before its scheduled liftoff.

This very visible sign of progress was a huge boost for NASA, which over the years had endured numerous criticisms of its space policy in general and the shuttle program in particular. As Columbia was inched toward its launch pad, gleaming brightly in the searchlights, validation seemed close at hand. Robert Frosch, NASA's Director at the time, went so far as to say, "We are now at the threshold of a new capability to investigate the universe."

This would be the first launch since 1975, when a Saturn 1B rocket had flown a U.S. crew to dock with a Russian Soyuz vehicle, and NASA was happy to be back in business. But first, Columbia had to cover the three and a half miles to the launch pad, a feat which took seven and a half hours on the lumbering Transporter. The original plan had been to launch an average of one shuttle a week, but it had already become obvious that such a schedule could never be met. Still, as Columbia stood proudly on its launch pad, workers swarming around to prepare the ship for its first flight, the sky no longer seemed to be the limit.

Selected to command the first flight was former Navy pilot John Young, an Apollo and Gemini veteran who, at 50, was considered one of the Grand Old Men of the space program. In the pilot's seat would be 43-year-old Robert Crippen, a Navy Captain and jet pilot. Between them, the two men had more than 12,000 hours of flight time. They had begun shuttle training in 1978, studying 25 hours a week and spending some 1,200 hours in sophisticated flight simulators that could reproduce any problem Columbia might have on her maiden journey.

On the morning of April 10, 1981, Columbia was poised on the pad, and seemed ready to fly. But a 40-millisecond timing difference between the craft's four onboard computers caused an abort signal, and the launch was scrubbed. When launch director George Page informed Young of the problem, the astronaut was unruffled. "George, shucks, these things are going to happen," Young told him. "We're ready to go tomorrow."

The launch was actually delayed two days, but on April 12 Young and Crippen were once again strapped into their seats, looking skyward through Columbia's windshield as they lay on their backs far above the pad. On the beaches, roadsides and rooftops near Kennedy Space Center, half a million people waited, squinting into the rising sun as they strained to catch a glimpse of the shuttle.

With 11 minutes to go and the launch sequence running smoothly, President Ronald Reagan transmitted a message to the crew: "We are the first and we are the best. We are so because we are free. As you hurtle from Earth in a craft unlike any other ever constructed, you will do so in a feat of American technology and will. As you embark on this daring enterprise, the hopes and prayers of all Americans are with you. May God bless you and bring you home safely."

Hugh Harris, the voice of Mission Control, began the countdown and marked off the seconds: "T-minus one minute, marked and counting . . . T-minus 45 seconds and counting . . ." At the 10-second mark, thousands of onlookers counted down along with the flight controller: "Nine, eight, seven, six, five, four, three, two, we're go on main engines, one . . ." and then Harris' words were drowned in a deafening chorus of cheers as Columbia rose majestically out of swirling smoke and flames and climbed toward the heavens.

Their mission accomplished, the launch team erupted in shouts and whistles, a few even waving small American flags. "God, what a beautiful sight to see," said one jubilant technician as he watched Columbia through the floor-to-ceiling windows of the firing room. As tension evaporated at the Kennedy Space Center, it was reaching its height in Houston as the Johnson Space Center took over the job of monitoring Columbia.

The spacecraft took only eight seconds to clear the launch tower and begin the roll maneuver that would put it in the proper trajectory for orbit. First-time astronaut Crippen's pulse soared to 130 beats per minute during ascent — especially when a piece of debris bounced off his windshield — but veteran Young's heart rate reached only 85. He would later joke that at his age, that's as fast as it would go.

At two minutes and 10 seconds into the flight, Columbia's solid rocket boosters separated from the external tank as planned and floated on parachutes to a water landing just 18 miles from the recovery ships. Six minutes after that, the ship's three main engines shut down right on time. Columbia had reached orbit.

The first item of business for Young and Crippen was to open the 60-foot cargo bay doors. The doors contain radiators that expel excess heat so getting them open as quickly as possible is always a priority once a shuttle reaches orbit. If, for some reason, the doors cannot be opened, flight rules dictate that the mission be aborted.

Fortunately, the doors opened smoothly and without incident. But cameras on Columbia's mid-deck that were recording the procedure showed a potentially dangerous problem: several of the heat-absorbing silica tiles were missing from the shuttle's Orbital Maneuvering System (OMS) pods, which are located on both sides of the tail. As Young put it in his calm drawl, "We want to tell y'all we do have a few tiles missing. I see one full square and looks like a few little triangular shapes that are missing."

Reassuringly, Young and Crippen could see the Nomex felt underlayment in the exposed areas, which meant there had been no breach of the hull. Furthermore, the OMS pods were shielded from the heat of re-entry by the shuttle's bulk, and flight engineers doubted there would be any danger from those particular missing tiles when the ship returned to Earth. They couldn't be sure about the bottom, but later speculation indicated that an Air Force spy satellite may have captured close-up pictures of the shuttle's underbelly and laid NASA's fears to rest, though that remains unsubstantiated. The Department of Defense has said it assisted the agency in checking the spacecraft, but citing "security considerations," would not explain exactly how that was accomplished.

With the exception of a couple of minor occurrences, the mission itself was uneventful. Young and Crippen spent their waking hours checking out the spacecraft's systems and recording data. On one occasion, though, a flight data recorder mysteriously stopped working, and the astronauts were unable to pry it open for repair. Then, during sleep periods, little things went awry. During their first sleep period the cabin temperature suddenly dropped to 37 degrees F. and Mission Control had to "turn up the thermostat," signaling a computer to send more hot water into Columbia's heating system so the astronauts wouldn't have to "break out the long undies," as one of them joked. During the second sleep period an alarm went off, indicating that a heating unit on one of Columbia's auxiliary power units had failed. The APUs control the landing gear and elevons, and rely on the heater to keep their fuel from freezing. It turned out to be a false alarm, and STS-1's amazing success record remained intact.

After 50 or so hours in orbit, the crew prepared Columbia to come home. To return through the atmosphere, space shuttles must turn around so that they're flying "backward," opposite to their direction of travel. The Orbital Maneuvering System engines then fire, slowing the spacecraft and allowing it to begin to drop from orbit. After the de-orbit burn, the pilot turns the ship so it once again faces forward and pitches the nose up to around 30 degrees so the underbelly can take the full brunt of the searing heat from atmospheric friction. During its first mission, Columbia was still an untested re-entry vehicle. Happily, Columbia's re-entry performance was impeccable. As it roared back into the atmosphere high over Big Sur at seven times the speed of sound, Crippen exclaimed, "What a way to come to California!" Interestingly, the astronauts' heart rates were the reverse of their liftoff levels during the return: Young's, which had been so low during liftoff, raced at 130 beats per minute during landing, while Crippen's rose to only 85. Perhaps one reason for Young's escalated rate was that the pilot gets only one chance to get the landing right; the space shuttle doesn't have the go-around capability that airliners do.

Certainly that's why Edwards Air Force base, with its miles of dry, flat lakebed, was chosen for the first landing. There's plenty of room for maneuvering, and if anything went wrong, the base's isolated location ensured minimal casualties on the ground. It turned out that John Young didn't need all that extra room. As Columbia lined up with the runway for final approach, the crowd gathered at Edwards breathlessly watched the big space plane plummet toward the ground at an angle seven times steeper than an airliner's descent. Just 19 seconds before touchdown, Young flared Columbia to a shallow nose-up angle and dropped the landing gear. The delta-winged craft, dubbed the "flying brickyard" because of its tiles, looked more like a butterfly as Young lowered it gently toward the runway. Flying closely beside and slightly behind Columbia, the pilot of a T-38 Talon chase plane counted off the final feet till touchdown. As the rear landing gear kissed the lakebed, Landing Team Flight Director Don Puddy, hundreds of miles away in Houston's Mission Control, instructed his charges to "prepare for exhilaration!" Nine seconds later, its nose gear settling softly onto the runway, Columbia was home.

For the first time since Apollo, the space program was front and center in America. Columbia's wildly successful first mission was taken by some as proof of the country's technological superiority, while others viewed it as the first step in uniting humankind in space. Whatever the reason, interest in space and space travel hit an all-time high following STS-1. Forgotten were the years of trouble with tiles and exploding engines. Even the shuttle program's budget overruns of more than 30 percent were ignored as the nation celebrated its celestial triumph.

And Columbia wasn't through. In its 22-year lifetime it set several records, was upgraded numerous times and became the workhorse of the shuttle fleet. Here are just a few of Columbia's many milestones:

STS-5 — November 11, 1982
Vance D. Brand, Commander
Robert F. Overmyer, Pilot

Joseph P. Allen, Mission Specialist
William Lenoir, Mission Specialist

STS-5 was the first operational Shuttle mission. The crew deployed two commercial communications satellites, ANIK C-3 for TELESAT Canada and SitS-C for Satellite Business Systems. The first spacewalk of the shuttle program was scheduled for the mission, but was cancelled when a spacesuit malfunctioned.

STS-9 — November 28, 1983
John W. Young, Commander
Brewster W. Shaw, Jr., Pilot
Owen K. Garriott, Mission Specialist
Dr. Robert A. R. Parker, Mission Specialist
Dr. Byron K. Lichtenberg, Payload Specialist
Dr. Ulf Merbold (European Space Agency), Payload Specialist

John Young returned to space on STS-9, which was also the first mission to feature the Spacelab module, a space laboratory carried in the shuttle's cargo bay. The Spacelab module was employed to conduct experiments in astronomy and physics as well as several other disciplines. On this mission Dr. Ulf Merbold became the first European Space Agency astronaut to fly on the shuttle.

STS-61C — January 12, 1986
Robert L. Gibson, Commander
Charles F. Bolden, Jr., Pilot
Franklin R. Chang-Diaz, Mission Specialist
Steven A. Hawley, Mission Specialist
Dr. George D. Nelson, Mission Specialist
Robert J. Cenker, Payload Specialist
Congressman Bill Nelson, Payload Specialist

NASA later abandoned the odd mission-numbering scheme adopted with STS-61C, but this mission is best known as the first space flight of an American Congressman. An RCA Americom satellite, SATCOM KU-I, was also deployed.

STS-32 — January 9, 1990
Daniel C. Brandenstein, Commander
James Wetherbee, Pilot
Dr. Bonnie J. Dunbar, Mission Specialist
Marsha S. Ivins, Mission Specialist
G. David Low, Mission Specialist

The STS-32 mission deployed the SYNCOM IV-F5 defense satellite. Columbia also retrieved the Long Duration Exposure Facility (LDEF), an experiment which had been left in space by a previous crew to determine the reaction of several materials to the environment of space.

STS-35 — December 2, 1990
Vance D. Brand, Commander
Guy S. Gardner, Pilot
John M. Lounge, Mission Specialist
Jeffery A. Hoffman, Mission Specialist
Dr. Robert A. Parker, Mission Specialist
Dr. Ronald A. Parise, Payload Specialist
Dr. Samuel T. Durrance, Payload Specialist

The ASTRO-1 observatory, made up of four telescopes and housed in Columbia's payload bay, was used to examine celestial targets in the ultraviolet and X-ray bands of the spectrum.

STS-40 — June 5, 1991
Bryan O. O'Connor, Commander
Sydney M. Gutierrez, Pilot
Dr. M. Rhea Seddon, Payload Commander
Dr. James P. Bagian, Mission Specialist
Dr. Tamara E. Jerrigan, Mission Specialist
Dr. F. Drew Gaffney, Payload Specialist
Dr. Millie Hughes-Fulford, Payload Specialist

The first shuttle mission devoted entirely to life sciences, STS-40 also marked the fifth use of the Spacelab module. Aboard were thousands of small jellyfish and 30 rats which the crew examined to study changes brought about by weightlessness, and to test a new animal containment system. They also studied their own cardiovascular/cardiopulmonary, renal/endocrine, musculoskeletal, neurovestibular, blood and immune systems for changes caused by microgravity.

STS-55 — April 26, 1993
  Steven R. Nagel, Commander
  Terence T. Henricks, Pilot
  Charles Precourt, Mission Specialist
  Dr. Bernard Harris, Jr., Mission Specialist
  Dr. Ulrich Walter, Payload Specialist
  Hans Schlegel, Payload Specialist

STS-55 marked the largest international cooperative mission thus far. Columbia carried 88 experiments prepared by eleven nations including the U.S., Germany, Japan, France and other members of the European Space Agency.

STS-75 — February 22, 1996
  Andrew M. Allen, Commander
  Scott J. Horowitz, Pilot
  Franklin R. Chang-Diaz, Payload Commander
  Maurizio Cheli, Mission Specialist
  Jeffrey A. Hoffman, Mission Specialist
  Claude Nicollier, Mission Specialist
  Umberto Guidoni, Payload Specialist

STS-75 carried the third U.S. Microgravity Payload experiment, but is more memorable for the experimental space tether it deployed. Called the Tether Satellite System Reflight, or TSS-1R, the experiment ended in failure when the tether broke.

$$* * *$$

As the oldest orbiter in the fleet, Columbia was the first shuttle to need an overhaul. In August 1991, it was brought to Rockwell International's facility in Palmdale, California for an extensive inspection and refit. Some 50 modifications were made, including the addition of carbon brakes, a drag chute, improved nose wheel steering, the removal of development flight instrumentation and an enhancement of its thermal protection system. By February 1992, the ship was back at Kennedy Space Center, ready for flight.

Almost 90 more changes were made when Columbia was brought back to Palmdale for further modification in 1994. Among them were upgrades of the main landing gear thermal barrier, tire pressure monitoring system and radiator drive circuitry as well as intensive structural inspections and the application of an upgraded corrosion control coating on the wings and rudder.

Columbia returned to the facility for the last time in 1999. Nearly 100 modifications were made, including the addition of a multi-functional electronic display system (MEDS) or "glass cockpit," which had already been fitted to the other ships in the fleet.

With all the years of tender loving care, Columbia seemed fit and healthy on the eve of STS-107's launch. Still, it was 22 years old, and the question remains: had it been enough?

Chapter 6
Fallen Heroes

The American space program is one of humankind's most impressive scientific triumphs. In less than a decade, following President John Kennedy's 1961 proclamation, the United States achieved the impossible by successfully landing two men on the moon and bringing them safely back home. From that remarkable accomplishment – a dream of man for millennia – sprang the space shuttle program, the International Space Station and much, much more.

But these achievements did not come without a price: over the past 36 years a total of 17 American astronauts have lost their lives in the line of duty. There have also been some near catastrophes, gripping events that tore at the hearts of the American people, kept them glued to their televisions and caused them to send up prayers for the safe return of the brave men who willingly risked their lives for the advancement of science.

From the moment we entered the space race, everyone knew that the ultimate price would likely be paid sometime. No matter how much care is given to the creation of spacecraft and the training of those who fly them, accidents still happen. Equipment fails; unforseen forces exert their influence; men and women die.

Exploration of the unknown has never been without risk — not since men set out into uncharted waters in fragile wooden ships in search of new lands. We continue to explore the uncharted today, only it's not blue and wet — it's vast and empty and cold.

Lives will always be lost in the pursuit of knowledge, but they're never lost in vain. Someone must take those first daring steps so that others may follow.

* * *

APOLLO 1

The United States entered the space race already behind. The Soviet Union had caused the country great embarrassment — and instilled more than a little fear — by successfully placing a man-made object, a basketball-sized satellite called Sputnik, into Earth orbit on

October 4, 1957. Less than a month later, Sputnik II was launched with a living payload, a dog named Laika, who would give her life for scientific pursuit.

Despite many failures, the United States eventually caught up with the Soviets, only to fall behind when the Soviet Union sent the first human — cosmonaut Yuri Gagarin — into space on April 12, 1961. Gagarin completed one orbit then returned safely to Earth. Back on the ground, he crowed, "Now let other countries try to catch us."

The United States readily rose to the challenge. The Soviet Union may have placed the first human in space, but the United States was determined to place the first man on the moon.

Alan Shepherd became the first American in space on May 5, 1961, just a month after Yuri Gagarin had made his historic flight. Shepherd's sub-orbital Mercury mission aboard Freedom 7 lasted just 15 minutes, but proved the United States was still in the race and gaining ground. Other successes followed — more Mercury flights, then the Gemini program. But it was the Apollo program that brought the moon within America's reach.

Apollo 1 was accepted by NASA in August 1966. It had taken North American Aviation Corp. two years to build. There had been frequent design changes along the way, followed by additional problems once NASA took possession.

Astronaut Virgil "Gus" Grissom, a veteran of the Mercury and Gemini programs, was named commander of Apollo 1. Accompanying him was Ed White, also a veteran of the Gemini program, and Roger Chaffee, a rookie who, at age 31, was the youngest member of the crew.

NASA was desperate to launch Apollo 1, an orbital flight designed to test the new spaceship in preparation for an eventual trip to the moon, and hoped to do so in November 1966. Unfortunately, technical problems forced the date to be pushed back until January 1967.

While the technical problems were being resolved, Grissom, White and Caffee honed their skills aboard a spacecraft trainer at Cape Kennedy. But Grissom wasn't pleased with the simulator. He felt it wasn't good enough, and once displayed his displeasure by hanging a lemon from it.

Even as NASA rectified them, the list of problems grew and grew: the radio system glitched, the oxygen and water supply systems were balky. This pushed the launch of Apollo 1 back yet again to February 26, 1967. Gus Grissom's frustration with the whole thing intensified.

The problems with Apollo 1 should have

come as no surprise to anyone. At the time, Project Apollo was one of the most complicated scientific and engineering programs ever devised, employing 300,000 individuals and 20,000 companies. The spacecraft contained nearly two million working parts. Simply put, scientists had been instructed to create the possible out of the impossible, and they had succeeded.

Joseph F. Shea, the spacecraft manager, was quite candid about the ship's problems in the December before the scheduled launch. Continued testing had found additional problems, but not all of them were cause for alarm. Shea said there were two types of problems — those that had to be fixed and those that didn't quite meet design specifications. NASA was forced to adopt a unique policy: run the program in a balanced way, but don't try to make everything too perfect or too complex. Otherwise, the job would never get done.

Additional problems were encountered in the huge Saturn V rocket, the monstrous beast that would hurl the Apollo craft to the moon with the power of more than 500 jet fighters. In one early test, a second stage engine exploded because someone had failed to connect some switches. In another, the third stage engine exploded because a piece of welding filler had been short of specifications.

Nonetheless, NASA was under the gun, so Apollo 1 was taken to Launch Complex 34 on January 6, 1967 in anticipation of a February launch. But even then, more problems emerged. Testing quickly ran behind schedule, so to save time NASA officials decided to skip a preliminary test that would have overfilled the capsule with a 100 percent oxygen atmosphere before the astronauts entered the craft.

It would prove to be a fatal error.

On the morning of January 27, a Friday, the Apollo 1 capsule sat atop a Saturn 1B rocket, surrounded by a service structure and encased in a clean room. Everything was ready for a launch simulation, an important step in determining whether the spacecraft would be ready to blast off as scheduled the following month. The task at hand was known as a "plugs out" test. All electrical, environmental and ground checkout cables would be disconnected to prove that the spacecraft and launch vehicle could function only on internal power after the umbilical lines dropped out.

By 8 a.m., an army of technicians 1,000 strong was checking systems to make sure everything was okay before pulling the plugs. In the blockhouse, the clean room, the service structure, the swing arm of the umbilical tower and the Manned Spacecraft Operations Building swarms of technicians were going through all the steps necessary to make sure that the ship was ready and able to carry its three-man crew into Earth's orbit. Twenty-five technicians worked on level A-8 of the service structure next to the command module and five more, most of them employees of North American Aviation Corp., were busy inside the clean room at the end of the swing arm. If interruptions and delays caused the test to go long, which happened often, round-the-clock shifts were ready to carry the exercise to completion. Most of the pre-boarding preparations went very smoothly, with one group after another finishing its checklist and reporting readiness.

After an early lunch, Grissom, White and Chaffee suited up and were taken to the pad, arriving a little after 1 p.m. Aided by technicians, they slid into their couches and made themselves as comfortable as possible within the ship's close confines. Technicians sealed the pressure vessel inner hatch, secured the outer crew access hatch, then locked the booster cover cap in place. Each of the astronauts had biomedical sensors on their bodies, tied together on the communications circuit and attached to the environmental control system. Strapped down, as they would be during a real launch, they purged their spacesuits and the cabin of all gases except oxygen, a standard operating procedure.

Grissom and his crew had spent nearly a year with the craft, watching it go through production, testing and launch pad preparations. After participating in numerous critiques, reading various discrepancy reports and participating in several suited trials in the craft, the men knew the ship as well as they knew their own homes. They were familiar with the capsule's 88 subsystems and had memorized the proper positions for the hundreds of switches and controls that covered the cockpit. They also knew that the environmental unit had been causing some problems, and one of Grissom's first comments upon entering the craft was about a strange odor he said smelled like sour milk.

As the test progressed, the cabin's atmosphere was replaced with pure oxygen at a pressure of 16.7 pounds per square inch. The crew checked lists, listened to the countdown and complained of communication problems that forced occasional delays. Somewhere was an unattended live microphone that could not be tracked down and turned off. Other systems, however, appeared to be functioning normally. At 4 p.m., a shift of technicians went home and another came on duty.

As day faded to night, communications problems again forced a 10-minute delay before the plugs could be pulled. The test was way behind schedule, and they still had to practice the emergency escape procedure. The astronauts were used to waiting, however, having gone through the same thing on trouble-plagued training simulators.

Many eyes and ears were trained on the capsule as the test progressed. Approximately half a mile away, Donald "Deke" Slayton, who along with Grissom was one of the original Mercury Seven, sat at a console in the blockhouse next to Stuart Roosa, the capsule communicator. Gary Propst, an RCA employee, was on the first floor of the launch complex watching a television monitor that had its camera trained on the window of the command module. Clarence A. Chauvin, the Kennedy Space Center Test Conductor, waited in the automated checkout equipment room of the operations building, and Darrell O. Cain, the North American Test Conductor, sat next door.

NASA Quality Control Inspector Henry H. Rogers boarded the Pad 34 elevator to ride up to the clean room. In the clean room were three North American employees: Donald O. Babbitt, the Pad Leader; James D. Gleaves, a mechanical engineer; and L. D. Reece, a systems technician who was waiting for the signal to pull the plugs. Just outside on the swing arm, Steven B. Clemmons and Jerry W. Hawkins were listening for Reece to call them to come help.

At 6:31 p.m., all hell broke loose as Clemmons, Hawkins, Reece and several others heard a frantic cry from Chaffee over the radio circuit: "We've got a fire in the spacecraft!"

Babbitt looked up from his desk, stunned. "Get them out of there!" he shouted. As Babbitt reached toward a squawk box to notify the blockhouse, a sheet of flame flashed from the spacecraft, its concussion hurling Babbitt toward the door. Terrified, Babbitt, Gleaves, Reece and Clemmons fled, but returned seconds later. Choking and gasping for air, all four men made several attempts to remove the spacecraft's hatches in a desperate bid to reach the men inside, but heat and smoke made the job impossible.

On the first floor of the launch complex, Propst's television showed a bright glow inside the capsule, followed by flames flaring around the window. The fire intensified for almost three minutes, feeding on the pure oxygen and flammable materials inside the capsule. Before the room housing the spacecraft filled with smoke, Propst watched, horrified, as the television showed silver-clad arms fumbling to open the ship's hatch.

"Blow the hatch!" Propst cried in frustration. "Why don't they blow the hatch?" Propst wouldn't learn until later that the hatch could not be opened explosively.

Slayton and Roosa also watched the horror show in slow-motion on their monitors, unable to help as smoke and fire filled the capsule and then the clean room. Roosa tried again and again to communicate with the craft, while Slayton screamed for the two physicians in the blockhouse to hurry to the pad.

In the clean room, Babbitt, Gleaves, Reese, Hawkins and Clemmons, now joined by Rogers, continued to brave the fire despite blistering heat and choking smoke. Every now and then, one would quickly leave the room to gasp for breath, then return to continue the fight. One by one, they were able to remove the booster cover cap and the outer and inner hatches, finally prying the last hatch open more than five minutes after the alarm had sounded. Blinded by smoke, they could only feel for the astronauts inside. There was no sign of life.

By the time the firemen arrived, the air had cleared to reveal a grisly scene. Roger Chaffee was still in his couch, but Grissom and White, apparently struggling to open the hatch as the flames roared around them, were so intertwined below the hatch sill that rescue workers couldn't tell who was who.

Fourteen minutes after the first cry of fire, physicians G. Fred Kelly and Alan C. Harter finally reached the smoldering clean room. They had difficulty removing the bodies from the capsule because the astronauts' suits had fused with molten nylon inside the craft.

NASA officials immediately cleared all unnecessary personnel, posted guards and called staff photographers to chronicle the nightmarish scene. Doctors labored throughout the night to remove the astronauts from the charred spaceship. Following an autopsy, the coroner reported that the astronauts had died within the first 18 seconds of the fire from asphyxiation caused by inhaling toxic gases. They had second and third degree burns on their bodies, but the coroner concluded that they were not severe enough to have caused death.

The Apollo 1 tragedy stunned the world and cast a pall over the Apollo program. Memorial services for Grissom, White and Chaffee were held in Houston on January 30. Grissom and Chaffee were buried at Arlington National Cemetery, and White was buried at the Military Academy at West Point.

An inquiry was launched immediately to find out what had caused the fire and to determine what safety measures would be needed to insure the safety of future Apollo astronauts. Floyd L. Thompson, director of Langley Research Center, was asked by NASA Administrator James Webb to head the inquiry. An official review board was formed soon after.

The board established tight security at

Complex 34, impounded important documents related to the accident and collected eye-witness reports. Not surprisingly, the national press was all over the story, reporting innuendo and rumor when facts were unavailable. Everyone assumed that answers would be easy to find and that NASA would have a full explanation within a couple of weeks, but such was not the case. By February 3, NASA officials realized that no single cause of the accident could immediately be found.

As part of the investigation, an Apollo capsule nearly identical to the one in which the astronauts had died was shipped from California to Florida, where it was dismantled for comparison with the dissected remains of Apollo 1.

Although the review board was not able to conclusively determine what triggered the fire, it was able to identify the conditions which lead to the disaster:

1. A sealed cabin, pressurized with an oxygen atmosphere.
2. An extensive distribution of combustible materials in the cabin.
3. Vulnerable wiring carrying spacecraft power.
4. Vulnerable plumbing carrying a combustible and corrosive coolant.
5. Inadequate provisions for the crew to escape.
6. Inadequate provisions for rescue or medical attention.

In the end, the board concluded, NASA's race to place a man on the moon had resulted in the agency focusing on technical issues over the mundane but equally important questions of crew safety. As a result, considerable changes were made in capsule design and testing to address the safety issues. Changes were also made to the lunar lander after investigators realized that the same problems that plagued the command module — the ship that takes the astronauts to the moon — were also in the craft that would take them to and from the lunar surface.

The Apollo 1 accident was a tragedy, but those involved — particularly the astronauts — were aware that there were dangers. Shortly before the mission, Gus Grissom said during an interview: "If we die, we want people to accept it. We are in a risky business and we hope that if anything happens to us, it will not delay the program. The conquest of space is worth the risk of life."

✳ ✳ ✳

APOLLO 13

The remarkable return of three astronauts aboard the crippled Apollo 13 spacecraft had become an ancient memory to most Americans when Ron Howard and Tom Hanks revived the heroic adventure in the 1995 movie of the same name. Sticking pretty close to the facts, the movie vividly portrayed both the hazards of lunar exploration and the never-say-die spirit of NASA's astronauts and support personnel.

The real story, of course, is the stuff of legend.

Apollo 13 was supposed to be the fifth flight to the moon and the third to carry men to the lunar surface. Its crew consisted of Commander James A. Lovell Jr., Command Module Pilot John L. Swigert and Lunar Module Pilot Fred W. Haise Jr.

The mission began at 2:13 p.m. EST on April 11, 1970 with a flawless launch from Cape Canaveral, Florida and continued without incident until the evening of April 13. Using a hand-held videocamera, the crew broadcast a television show for the folks back home. Unfortunately, the space program had become so routine by then that few of the networks opted to carry it. Nonetheless, the astronauts had fun, hamming it up and showing viewers the interior of the command module, a conical compartment called Odyssey that measured just 13 feet by 10 feet and which served as their home for the duration of their journey. Attached to the command module was the cylindrical service module, which contained the electrical system, oxygen tanks and other equipment. Attached to the front of the craft was the lunar module, Aquarius, which was to take Lovell and Haise to the moon's surface and back.

With Lovell holding the camera, Haise gave a brief tour of Aquarius, demonstrating various equipment. The 49-minute broadcast concluded with Lovell saying, "This is the crew of Apollo 13 wishing everybody there a nice evening, and we're just about ready to close out our inspection of Aquarius and get back for a pleasant evening in Odyssey. Good night." Haise and Lovell rejoined Swigert in the command module.

At a few minutes after 9 p.m., a yellow caution light began flashing over the astronauts' heads, indicating low pressure in one of the hydrogen tanks in the service module. At Mission Control in Houston, a similar light began flashing on the console of a systems operations engineer named Seymour Liebergot, whose job was to monitor the electrical and environmental systems in the command module.

The hydrogen tank was part of the system used to generate electricity and water. It was science at its simplest — hydrogen combined with oxygen in the fuel cells to generate electricity, and in so doing, also generated drinkable water. The system had plenty of built-in redundancy: two hydrogen tanks, two oxygen tanks and three fuel cells. If anything went wrong with one, the second provided an emergency backup.

Liebergot wasn't overly concerned about the low hydrogen warning, but it did present a more ominous problem: the warning preempted the circuits of the entire warning system, meaning that any subsequent problems would not be immediately noticed.

Around that time, Swigert was instructed to stir the oxygen tanks, a standard procedure. It went well for about 16 seconds, then things went horribly wrong. It would later be determined that an arc of electricity shot between two bare wires, heating the oxygen within the tank and causing the pressure to skyrocket.

The mounting pressure caused an explosion that blew the dome off the oxygen tank and set fire to the insulation between the inner and outer shells of the tank. The intense heat ignited the Mylar that lined the housing bay, producing gases that quickly blew off the bay cover.

In the command module, the astronauts were immediately aware that something had happened, but they weren't exactly sure what it was. Because of the vacuum of space, the explosion was not as noticeable as it might have been back on Earth. Lovell had heard a bang and Swigert had felt a shudder, all of which suggested that their mission was no longer flawless.

Swigert radioed Mission Control in Houston, his voice so calm that capsule communicator Jack Lousma was unsure for a moment who he was talking to. "Houston," Swigert said, "we have a problem here."

"This is Houston, say again please," Lousma replied.

Lovell repeated for Swigert: "Houston, we've had a problem."

Swigert and Lovell may have sounded calm, but the flight surgeon at Mission Control, who monitored heartbeat and other life signs of the three astronauts, knew otherwise. The pulse reading of the three crewmen had skyrocketed from 70 to 130 beats per minute in a matter of moments.

At Mission Control, engineers initially thought they were dealing with a simple instrumentation failure. But within a minute of the explosion, Lovell informed them that Main Bus B had no power at all, and Main Bus A was losing power at an alarming rate. The news confused Liebergot because the two main electrical buses drew their power from three redundant fuel cells. If one cell died, the others should pick up the slack. There was obviously a problem with Apollo 13's electrical system, but where?

It eventually became apparent that only one of the craft's three fuel cells was still functioning, and it was already showing signs of a slow drain. Of all the problems NASA engineers had dealt with in the Apollo program, this was one they had never encountered before.

Lovell said later that the crew's first emotions

weren't fear but disappointment because mission rules forbade a lunar landing with only one fuel cell. In an instant, their years of training and sacrifice became meaningless. The astronauts of Apollo 13 would never know the extraordinary thrill of leaving their footprints on the lunar surface.

At that moment, however, their very survival was at stake, and things were going from bad to worse very quickly. The explosion had caused the spaceship to wobble uncontrollably, despite the guidance computer and Lovell's manual efforts to bring it under control. It was as if something was pouring out of the ship and acting like a thruster which, in fact, was exactly what was happening — gases and debris were venting into space through the hole created by the explosion.

The wobbling posed a host of problems, including the possibility that the ship's guidance system would lock, making navigation impossible. There was also the issue of maintaining an even temperature over the ship's outer surface. The pitching and yawing interfered with radio communication because the antennas had to be pointed toward Earth to receive signals — and for one brief but frightening moment, communication with Mission Control ceased completely.

In an attempt to figure out what had

happened, flight director Eugene Krantz instructed Lovell to read all of the gauges related to the ship's electrical system. Lovell got as far as the oxygen tanks, then stopped. The pressure in tank number two was zero. Lovell glanced through the window leading into the service module, where he saw some kind of white vapor. "It looks to me like we're venting something," he radioed Mission Control. "We are venting something out into space." That was obviously the cause of the wobbling.

Though mission controllers didn't know it just yet, the oxygen that Lovell saw in the service module was a very bad sign. The explosion had ruptured tank number two and damaged pipes and valves so that oxygen was now leaking out of tank number one. Oxygen was necessary for the fuel cells to function — once it was depleted, the ship would be without electricity to power its many life support systems.

The astronauts were instructed to power down the command module in an attempt to lessen the strain on the remaining electrical bus. The systems had to be powered down in a specific sequence, which was listed in the Emergency Power-Down Checklist. But in order to find the checklist, the crew had to sacrifice precious minutes to search through nearly 20 pounds of instruction material.

In the end the power-down was successful, but

the power in the command module continued to drop. It was then that mission controllers realized just how serious the problem was. Once the command module lost all power, the crew of Apollo 13 would have to rely on the lunar module as a lifeboat if they were going to return home safely.

This wasn't a new concept. NASA had evaluated the lunar module as a lifeboat as early as 1962, but a study at the Manned Spacecraft Center concluded that there was no conceivable command module failure that would make it necessary. Apparently they were wrong.

Using the lunar module as a lifeboat posed some serious questions, however. For one thing, it was designed to support two men for two days, not three men for the four days it might take to return to Earth. In addition, the vehicle was not equipped with a heat shield, meaning it would have to be jettisoned before entering the Earth's atmosphere and the crew would have to find a way to fly the crippled command module. This was something that had never even been discussed, much less attempted, during preflight simulation.

Meanwhile, Mission Control was put on full alert as the extent of the damage became apparent. Extra tracking equipment was added to the usual network used to monitor each space flight, and additional computers were hooked up at the Goddard Space Flight Center in Maryland. In addition, the Real Time Computer Complex located on the ground floor operations wing was instructed to bring in a giant IBM computer so that data from the stricken craft could be processed immediately. "Failure is not an option," Krantz told his dedicated staff. If it was at all possible, Apollo 13 and its crew would return home safely.

The question was, should Apollo 13 circle the moon first, as many mission controllers argued, or try for a direct abort? It was finally decided to continue around the moon. With its velocity imparted by the huge Saturn V rocket, the craft was going so fast that a retro-burn would have used up most of its fuel, leaving very little for re-entry maneuvering. By using the moon's gravity to slingshot the module back to Earth, the crew lost some time but conserved fuel.

As Mission Control prepared for the long road ahead, Haise began to prepare the lunar module. While it contained many of the same instruments as the command module, it was considerably smaller. Haise pondered how they would fit three men into a compartment built for only two. Well, they'd manage. Of greater importance at that moment was powering up the craft, a difficult task because all of the checklists on board called for utilization of the command module which was losing power at a frighteningly rapid rate. Luckily, Mission Control was able to send instructions for powering up the lunar module using its own batteries.

Lovell followed Haise to the lunar module, leaving Swigert to turn off everything but the cabin lights, the radio, the guidance system and the heaters and fan inside oxygen tank number one. The heaters inside the craft's delicate guidance system were also left on because the astronauts were afraid that if the system became too cold, it might malfunction when they needed it the most — four days later when they entered Earth's atmosphere on the way home. With so little power left in the command module, however, the astronauts had no choice but to divert power for the guidance heaters from the lunar module.

With everything taken care of in the dying command module, Lovell, Swigert and Haise settled into the lunar module for the 20-hour swing around the moon. During those 20 hours, NASA engineers faced the daunting task of figuring out how to get the ship through re-entry and splashdown. The ship's present trajectory was expected to bring it around the moon and back toward the Earth, but the venting oxygen had severely affected its free return trajectory. On its present course, it would miss the Earth by nearly 40,000 miles.

Engineers tossed around a number of ideas on how to correct Apollo 13's course and finally determined that a couple of brief firings of the lunar module's main engine would return it to its proper trajectory. The first burn had to take place in the next couple of hours, with a second burn after the ship had rounded the moon.

No one was sure if the lunar module's main engine would fire, and they held their breath when Lovell pushed the button. Suddenly the men felt themselves being pressed against the module floor, the only indicator that the rocket had fired. At long last, something had gone right.

Back in Mission Control, NASA engineers were taking stock of the water, oxygen and electricity in the lunar module. Though everyone expected the return home to take less than the projected four days, it was agreed that the crew should conserve as much as they could, just to be safe.

The next problem that had to be addressed was the inevitable buildup of carbon dioxide in the lunar module. Ordinarily, the air in the command module and the lunar module is circulated through pellets of lithium hydroxide, which removes the toxic natural byproduct of breathing. The lithium hydroxide was stored in special canisters that had to be replaced when they became saturated with carbon dioxide, and there weren't enough canisters in the lunar module to make it all the way back to Earth. The command module had additional canisters, but they wouldn't fit the lunar module's system.

This was literally a matter of life and death. If the problem couldn't be corrected — and soon — Lovell, Swigert and Haise would die before they got home. A team of Crew Systems Engineers was handed the task and ordered to make it work. In essence, they were being asked to make a square peg fit in a round hole, with no margin for error.

Several astronauts arrived at the Control Center to offer their help in solving the myriad problems facing their friends aboard Apollo 13. Charles Duke took over a simulator to figure out how the disabled craft could be placed into a thermal roll — what astronauts called "barbecue mode" — so it wouldn't become too hot or too cold on the ride home. He finally determined that firing the thrusters in small bursts seemed to do the trick, and passed the information on to an exhausted Lovell, who finally was able to get the ship relatively stabilized and aimed in the right direction. He had to manually rotate the ship 90 degrees every hour, but it kept the temperatures even.

Next up was the issue of re-entry and landing. On its present course, the ship would splash down in the Indian Ocean, far from an available rescue ship. A fast burn would bring it down in the Pacific, where recovery ships were more plentiful. To make a fast burn happen, however, the service module would have to be jettisoned. It was a risky proposition because the service module was fitted over the command module's ceramic heat shield to protect the shield from the cold, and no one knew how exposure to the bitter temperatures of outer space would affect the shield during the last part of the journey. A second option was a slower burn, which would require an additional day but would allow the crew to keep the service module in place. Ultimately, that was the choice made by mission controllers.

Once Apollo 13 had rounded the moon, Lovell had to perform another burn to correct the errant trajectory. When Mission Control instructed him to hit the button, he held his breath until he felt the surge — it had worked!

Following the burn, Mission Control hoped to send the crew instructions for powering down the craft for the remainder of the flight so they could relax and get some rest. By then, Lovell, Swigert and Haise had been awake for nearly two full days, and they were feeling the strain. It was hard to think, their reflexes were slowing and Lovell was afraid they would make a crucial mistake.

But sleep continued to elude them when an

argument ensued between engineers who wanted to simply power down the speeding craft and those who believed a better thermal roll had to be established. The latter feared that some part of the craft might become too hot from exposure to the sun and fail at a crucial moment — and ultimately they won out. But Lovell found establishing a proper thermal roll anything but easy. Just when he thought he got it right, the ship would start to wobble again. Worse, there seemed to be another error in their trajectory caused by something in the craft venting into space.

But there was also some good news. The Crew Systems Engineers had developed a quick and effective method to cleanse the lunar module's atmosphere of carbon dioxide, which had built to dangerous levels. In fact, a yellow warning light had gone on informing the crew their air had almost run out. Once the fix was made the atmosphere improved and the warning light eventually went off.

As Apollo 13 drew closer to home, its trajectory continued to deteriorate. If not corrected quickly, the ship would pass the Earth and sail endlessly back into space. On Wednesday, April 15, the three astronauts prepared for a manual course-correcting burn. It was a delicate move with incredible implications — if it wasn't done just right, the crew would be doomed. It was a tense few minutes, but again the burn went well, returning them to a trajectory headed straight for Earth.

The craft was almost home, but the astronauts were extremely uncomfortable. With no power for heat, the temperature inside the lunar module had fallen to a bone-chilling 38 degrees F., which made sleep impossible. Fred Haise had developed a painful kidney infection and couldn't stop shivering. John Swigert had accidentally spilled water on his shoes two days earlier and still had cold, wet feet. The walls and windows of the module dripped with water from condensation. The astronauts briefly considered donning their bulky spacesuits, but that would only have increased their discomfort.

While the crew shivered and hankered for home, engineers at Mission Control had developed a useable checklist for re-entry, which was scheduled for noon on Friday, April 17. Under normal circumstances, such a checklist takes nearly three months, but with their friends' lives at stake, they had managed this miraculous feat in only three days.

Just 58,000 miles from home, the crew of Apollo 13 successfully performed one last, tiny course-correcting burn, despite their mental and physical exhaustion. When the time came for re-entry, they strapped themselves into the command module, which they powered up with the lunar module. The module was a "cold, clammy tin can," Lovell recalled. "The walls, ceiling, floor, wire harnesses and panels were all covered with droplets of water. We suspected conditions were the same behind the panels. The chances of short circuits caused us apprehension, to say the least. But thanks to the safeguards built into the command module after the disastrous fire in January 1967, no electrical arcing took place."

Four hours before landing, the crew jettisoned the service module. As they watched it slowly drift away, they saw for the first time the extent of the damage caused by the explosion — one entire panel was missing, and wreckage was hanging out. Three hours later, the lunar module — their lifeboat for almost four days — was cut loose. Though the accommodations had left a lot to be desired, the men were grateful. The module had saved their lives.

Re-entry was a nail-biter for the crew at Mission Control. They had done everything they could think of to make it work, but it was now in God's hands. Was the trajectory right? Would the heat shield hold up? As the command module entered the Earth's atmosphere, communication with the ship was lost. Mission controllers began counting down the seconds. More than a minute passed, and everyone feared the worst. Then, at 12:07 p.m., they heard

Swigert's weary voice: "Okay, Joe." Within minutes the USS Iwo Jima, which had been standing by, plucked the battered craft out of the blue Pacific.

Against all odds, Apollo 13 was home, its crew safe. With the tragedy averted, the world breathed a sigh of relief.

* * *

SPACE SHUTTLE CHALLENGER

Like the day President John Kennedy was assassinated, the day of the Challenger explosion remains forever burned into the world's collective psyche. It was NASA's first catastrophic event since the Apollo 1 fire, which had occurred 19 years earlier almost to the day, and the ensuing investigation and design modifications would ground the shuttle fleet for more than two years.

The morning of January 27, 1986 was particularly cold, especially for central Florida, where shorts, T-shirts and sandals were typical attire year-round. Challenger, which was about to make the historic 25th shuttle mission, sat majestically on its launch pad, while shivering spectators huddled in thick jackets, their faces covered by scarves, waiting for the ship to roar skyward.

NASA had been under extraordinary pressure from Congress and the American public to fulfill its promise of making the space shuttle a viable space taxi, but things had not gone well in recent months. Problems big and small had forced delays in earlier launches, and Challenger had faced four frustrating postponements of its own. Everyone was eager to get the mission underway, particularly the seven-member crew and their support staff at Mission Control in Houston.

This particular flight was special for a variety of reasons, the most notable being the inclusion of the first civilian into space, a pretty New Hampshire school teacher named Christa McAuliffe, who had won a nationwide "Teacher in Space" competition. McAuliffe viewed her participation in the space program as an exciting way to bring the wonders of science to young people around the world.

Accompanying McAuliffe was:

* Commander Francis (Dick) Scobee, a veteran astronaut who had been the pilot of STS-41-C, the fifth orbital flight of the Challenger space craft. During that mission, Scobee's crew had successfuly retrieved and repaired the ailing Solar Maximum Satellite and returned it to orbit.

* Pilot Michael J. Smith, a commander in the U.S. Navy, where he had flown fighter jets and worked as a test pilot. This was Smith's first shuttle mission.

✳ Mission Specialist Judith Resnik, who had the distinction of being the second American woman in orbit during the maiden flight of Discovery in 1984. During that mission, she helped deploy three satellites into orbit and was also involved in biomedical research.

✳ Mission Specialist Ronald E. McNair, who achieved the distinction of being the second black American in space as a crew member on an earlier Challenger mission in 1984.

✳ Mission Specialist Ellison S. Onizuka, an Air Force officer who had participated in the first dedicated Department of Defense classified mission aboard Columbia in 1985.

✳ Payload Specialist Gregory B. Jarvis, who worked for the Hughes Aircraft Corporation's Space and Communications Group in Los Angeles. He was accepted into the astronaut program in 1984 under Hughes' sponsorship after competing against 600 other employees for the opportunity.

At 11:38 a.m. EST, the countdown reached zero and Challenger's rockets were ignited, sending the enormous craft skyward. The air temperature at launch was 36 degrees F., 15 degrees colder than any previous launch. It was so cold that icicles could be seen hanging off buildings around the Kennedy Space Center.

The first few seconds of the launch seemed to go relatively smoothly. Onboard computers rolled the ship on its back while it ascended as planned. Strapped on their backs on two decks, the astronauts were rocked by the deafening noise and tremendous vibrations that always accompany liftoff. The force of acceleration pressed them against their couches, a sensation once described as "having a bear sit on your chest."

"Looks like we've got a lot of wind up here," said Smith over the intercom.

"Yeah," Scobee replied. He turned slightly in his couch. "It's a little hard to see out my window here."

Challenger exceeded Mach 1 — the speed of sound — at 19,000 feet. The onboard computers throttled back the three main engines to 65 percent of thrust in anticipation of the incredible aerodynamic stress placed on the ship.

"Okay, we're throttling down," Scobee said, as if to reassure the rookies on board. A few seconds later, the ship passed through some wind sheer, causing it to sway like a carnival ride.

"Throttle up," Scobee instructed, his eyes glued to the flight data screen in front of him.

"Throttle up," Smith confirmed.

"Roger," Scobee replied.

"Feel that mother go!" Smith yelled joyously as the shuttle accelerated. "Whoo hoo!"

In Houston, capsule communicator Richard

Covery watched the proceedings on his monitor, happy that everything seemed to be going well. "Challenger," he said, "go at throttle up."

"Roger," Scobee replied. "Go at throttle up."

Challenger was now 70 seconds into its historic flight, nearing 50,000 feet. The worst turbulence was behind them. Then, inexplicably and without warning, the ship shuddered violently.

"Uh oh," said Smith, his voice tinged with concern and apprehension.

In a heartbeat, all telemetry stopped. The screens in Mission Control showed only a white S, meaning the downlink had been severed. Challenger was gone. A moment passed, then another. Steve Nesbitt, the voice of Mission Control, finally spoke: "Flight controllers here looking very carefully at the situation. Obviously a major malfunction."

At Kennedy Space Center, cheers gave way to stunned silence as the craft appeared to explode in the sky above and three huge plumes of smoke arced in different directions. Those who had never witnessed a shuttle launch up close before were unsure what they had just seen. Were the plumes a natural aspect of launch? But the old hands knew immediately what the billowing white smoke meant. Seven brave men and women were dead and a $2 billion spacecraft had been blown to bits.

The day before the launch, several NASA engineers had expressed concerns over the frigid temperatures at Kennedy Space Center and what effect the cold might have on the space shuttle, particularly the rubber O-rings in the solid rocket boosters. The O-rings had never been tested in such low temperatures, and there was just no telling what effect the cold might have. However, space agency officials were feeling increasing pressure to get the mission underway as quickly as possible, so the concerns were dismissed and the decision to go ahead with the launch was confirmed the night before.

As it turns out, the engineers were right to be concerned. In ideal conditions, when the solid rocket boosters are ignited, the hot gases inside are supposed to cause the O-rings to expand in the casting joints, preventing flames from leaking out. But on that chilly January morning, the rubber rings had become frozen, so they took a fraction of a second longer to expand, a months-long investigation concluded. One set of O-rings on the right solid rocket booster immediately burned away, releasing a noticeable puff of black smoke immediately after liftoff.

The joint held for several more seconds, most likely because charred material was blocking the exit of exhaust through the side. But as the shuttle passed through the moment of maximum aerodynamic pressure — known as max-Q — the charred blockage was apparently dislodged and flame shot out the side of the booster. The gap in the casing opened a little bit more, causing the bottom of the booster to break free from the external tank. Almost instantly the nose of the solid rocket booster pierced the external tank causing liquid hydrogen and liquid oxygen to spew from their special pressurized tanks and burst into a tremendous fireball.

Part of the shooting plumes witnessed by spectators were the solid rocket boosters, which had been blown free by the force of the explosion and continued to fly uncontrollably. The shuttle broke into several large pieces and fell into the ocean, a terrifying trip that took more than two minutes. If the astronauts weren't killed by the force of the explosion or the shuttle's disintegration, they were certainly killed by the force of impact with the ocean.

The Challenger disaster was a devastating blow to NASA. Unlike the Apollo 1 fire, which had been witnessed by only a handful of people, the Challenger explosion was a horrifying public spectacle that shook the world to its core. It also reminded an increasingly complacent public that space exploration, no matter how routine it seemed, was a very risky endeavor.

In the aftermath of the disaster, all pending shuttle flights were immediately cancelled while a review board tried to figure out what had happened. NASA engineers had concluded within a few hours of the accident that the rubber O-rings were the primary factor, but it would take investigators months to confirm these suspicions.

Five months after the tragedy, a government commission concluded what most engineers already knew — the accident could have been avoided if only the space agency hadn't been in such a rush to launch.

Furious that their safety was being compromised for the sake of expedience, a few astronauts left the program. In addition, several top NASA officials were replaced. The next shuttle mission didn't take place until 1988.

While NASA and the American people have put the Challenger accident behind them, they have not forgotten its crew. Annual observances are held each year on the date of the tragedy to commemorate their heroic efforts. On January 16, 1996 — at the tenth anniversary of Challenger observance — NASA Administrator Daniel Goldin issued the following statement:

"The best way to honor the memories of the crew of the Challenger, and of all the men and women who have given their lives to explore the frontiers of air and space, is to continue their bold tradition of exploration and innovation. That's what the people of NASA do every day.

They push the boundaries of knowledge and human endeavor to improve and enrich life on Earth today and secure a better future for all of us tomorrow.

"I've said many times that safety is the highest priority at today's NASA. We will not waver from that commitment. But human beings have always taken great risks to reap great rewards. Space flight is inherently dangerous and every member of the NASA team understands those risks.

"I'm proud of the women and men of NASA. They're blazing the trail to the future. They're building the components of the International Space Station. They're constructing spacecraft that will explore the farthest regions of the solar system and the universe, and satellites that will monitor the health of our own blue planet for years to come. They're conducting cutting edge research that will make airplanes faster and safer, and they've made the space shuttle the most capable, reliable and versatile spacecraft in the world."

✳ ✳ ✳

THE LUCKY ONES

Apollo 13 was the near-disaster that the world remembers most vividly, but in fact there have been numerous heart-stoppers over the course of the American space program, beginning with John Glenn's historic three-orbit flight aboard the Mercury capsule Friendship 7 on February 20, 1962.

At the end of the first orbit, the automatic control system aboard the craft malfunctioned. NASA engineers had planned to let Glenn take brief manual control of the capsule as an experiment, but the malfunction forced him to pilot the ship manually during both the second and third orbits as well as re-entry. Luckily, the manual control system functioned extremely well, so Glenn was able to continue with the 5 hour and 55 minute flight.

During Glenn's second orbit, mission controllers learned that Friendship 7's heat shield had apparently come loose and that the only thing holding the shield to the capsule were the straps that held the rocket to the capsule. With the clock ticking, the engineers decided that the safest thing would be for Glenn to keep the retrorocket pack strapped to the capsule during re-entry, rather than jettisoning it as originally planned, and steer the capsule so that the pressure of the atmosphere would hold the heat shield in place during descent.

There was a brief radio blackout during Glenn's tricky re-entry and everyone in Mission Control held their breath as Friendship 7 plummeted through the Earth's atmosphere, the heat shield glowing bright red from atmospheric friction. When Glenn finally radioed that he had splashed down safely, the engineers at Mission Control heaved a collective sigh of relief.

There was another close call during the flight of Gemini 8 in March 1966. Astronauts David R. Scott and Neil Armstrong, who would go on to become the first man to set foot on the moon, docked with an Agena target vehicle as planned, but 27 minutes later a stuck thruster sent the combined craft into an unexpected and violent spin. The gyrations were so intense that the spacecraft was in danger of breaking apart and the astronauts were close to blacking out. Armstrong finally managed to undock from the Agena, thinking that was the cause of the problem, but in so doing only made the problem worse. Armstrong and Scott finally shut down the ship's main reaction control system and used the re-entry control system to slow the gyrations to zero.

The astronauts desperately wanted the mission to continue, but NASA ordered an emergency return and Gemini 8 successfully splashed down in the Pacific on March 16.

(Neil Armstrong appears to be one of the luckiest astronauts to don a spacesuit. In other close calls he was nearly killed while testing a jet-powered lunar lander simulator at Ellington Air Force Base in Texas in May 1968, and came perilously close to running out of fuel while landing the lunar module on the moon during Apollo 11.)

* * *

SOVIET SPACE DISASTERS

From the early days of the Cold War through the 1970s, the Soviet Union was very tight-lipped about every aspect of its space program. It was in a genuine race with the United States for space supremacy, and that meant keeping secrets.

As a result, numerous rumors quickly spread about unreported tragedies within the Soviet space program, including cosmonauts who perished in the cold depths of space when their ships malfunctioned, cosmonauts killed during secret attempts to reach the moon before the United States, and even cosmonauts lost during the fall of Soviet Communism as they attempted a desperate manual return from Mir.

Most of these rumors have been written off as the wild rantings of hardcore conspiracy theorists, but it's true that the Russian space program has experienced its share of tragedy.

On April 23, 1967, just three months after the Apollo 1 fire, the Soviet Union launched Soyuz 1, the first in a new generation of large spacecraft. At the controls was Col. Vladimir

Komarov, a veteran of the Soviet air force. The launch, per Soviet custom, was kept secret until after Komarov achieved orbit. In fact, Komarov's own wife didn't even know he was in space until notified by one of her husband's fellow pilots 25 minutes after the launch.

The mission, which American space officials believed was a docking experiment like many in NASA's Gemini series, went well at first. Komarov even sent greetings from space to his homeland and saluted "the courageous Vietnamese people fighting against the bandit aggression of American imperialism."

Then, about 27 hours after launch, the flight bulletins ceased. The Soviet people waited and worried for another 11 hours before being told that Komarov had been killed during re-entry when the parachutes on his craft malfunctioned. American officials felt the explanation was too convenient, that something disastrous must have happened to the ship in orbit, but there was no real way of finding out.

Whatever the reason, Vladimir Komarov became the first human to die in space and the Soyuz 1 accident affected the Soviet space program just as badly as Apollo 1 had stricken its American counterpart. The Soviet Union did not launch another Soyuz spaceship for 16 months.

Other nations currently persuing manned

spaceflight, such as China and Japan, will no doubt experience similar catastrophes over the course of their own endeavors. The death of good men and women is the tragic but inevitable price humankind must pay for the exploration of worlds unknown.

Chapter 7
Rethinking the Future

The giant rotating wheel first appears just over Earth's limb, its white flanks a stark contrast to the rust-colored girders of its still-unfinished sections. As spacesuited construction workers pause to watch, the flight crew aboard the incoming passenger liner engages the automatic rendezvous sequence, locking the needle-shaped spacecraft into an imaginary path aimed at the space station's hangar deck.

As the ship's computers begin to turn it to match the station's slow rotation, the two craft seem to perform a ballet in the airless void. The brightly-lit hangar looms ever larger in the flight deck's windows until the commercial spaceliner enters the docking bay, delivering its passengers to orbit.

This scene from the motion picture "2001: A Space Odyssey" was prophetic — As the year

2001 dawned, there was indeed an International Space Station in orbit around Earth. Although not as large as Stanley Kubrick and Arthur C. Clarke had envisioned in 1968, it is still a marvel of engineering and a tribute to the spirit of discovery that has always characterized humankind.

America's tradition of exploration goes all the way back to its first inhabitants, who roamed the prairies searching for food and discovering new hunting lands. With the landing of Christopher Columbus, the era of European exploration of the continent began, continued later by English settlers at Yorktown. Lewis and Clark's expedition later opened the western frontier, and the United States is now populated from sea to sea.

There were many reasons why immigrants left their homelands for the New World, or families in covered wagons departed the only civilization they knew to trek westward toward the unknown. But they all shared one pervasive trait: mankind's innate need to explore.

The going was rarely easy. In the early 1600s, the Jamestown settlement was nearly wiped out by disease. And in the 20-year period between 1835 and 1855 during the westward expansion, more than 10,000 people died on the Oregon Trail alone, usually from firearms accidents, cholera or smallpox. And yet, the settlers kept coming.

Just as those early travelers understood that there was no guarantee they would reach their destinations alive, astronauts and cosmonauts know full well the risks of their chosen profession. As Columbia prepared to lift off for the first time, the world held its collective breath, waiting to see if this new flying machine would prove spaceworthy.

But as the years went by and shuttle flights became more common, we gave way to complacency. Shuttle launches were given a paragraph or two in the paper or a minute of coverage on the evening news. To the public, spaceflight had become routine.

But it was never routine for the people who flew those missions. Better than anyone, they understood the explosive potential of the liquid hydrogen and liquid oxygen fuels that make the shuttle a potential bomb. They knew that the solid rocket boosters, once lit, could not be turned off. And they knew that even a single micrometeorite strike in orbit could spell their doom. With a flying machine as complex as the space shuttle, there were many ways to die. And yet they not only flew the fire-breathing monster into space repeatedly, but competed for the privilege even after the Challenger disintegrated in the skies over the Kennedy Space Center in 1986.

After Challenger, naysayers emerged from the

woodwork with their I-told-you-so's, claiming that human spaceflight was much too dangerous. Unmanned robots could explore both the solar system and the near-Earth environment without risking human life, they said, pointing to successful space probes such as Voyagers I and II as proof.

And they were partly right.

Exploring space is a dangerous business. As we continue to expand our influence beyond our planet, there will undoubtedly be more accidents, more loss of life. But if you ask the intrepid men and women whose lives are in the balance, you will not find a single one who would suggest we turn away from the human exploration of the cosmos. As Navy Rear Admiral Grace Murray Hopper once noted, "A ship in port is safe — but that's not what ships are built for."

The day after Columbia's tragic end, Laurel Clark's brother was asked to comment on the continuance of the space program. "We certainly all hope NASA keeps going and continues on with its mission," he said. "I think it's very important for humanity to keep this going." A few days later, Grace Corrigan, mother of Challenger astronaut/teacher Christa McAuliffe, echoed the sentiment. "There's a risk in it, and there will always be a risk in it," she said, "but there's no reason to shut the program down. It's done too much for humanity. If we didn't continue, they (the astronauts) would have died in vain."

Just two days after the accident, the families of Columbia's crew issued a joint statement: "On January 16th, we saw our loved ones launch into a brilliant, cloud-free sky. Their hearts were full of enthusiasm, pride in country, faith in their God, and a willingness to accept risk in the pursuit of knowledge — knowledge that might improve the quality of life for all mankind.

"Columbia's 16-day mission of scientific discovery was a great success, cut short by mere minutes — yet it will live on forever in our memories. We want to thank the NASA family and people from around the world for their incredible outpouring of love and support.

"Although we grieve deeply, as do the families of Apollo 1 and Challenger before us, the bold exploration of space must go on. Once the root cause of this tragedy is found and corrected, the legacy of Columbia must carry on — for the benefit of our children and yours."

On the day of the disaster, President George W. Bush reiterated his continued support for the space program in a speech from the White House Cabinet Room: "The cause in which they died will continue. Mankind is led into the darkness beyond our world by the inspiration of discovery and the longing to understand. Our journey into space will go on."

In the aftermath of NASA's second in-flight space disaster, it's obvious the majority of Americans still want a space program. But exactly how we will recover from the latest shuttle tragedy and what the program will look like afterward is uncertain. Columbia was an amazing spaceship — but it was 22 years old. Most automobiles last less than half that long, let alone a craft that is expected to blast into orbit in one long controlled explosion, operate as a spacecraft for several days and then return to Earth as a glider, braving blast-furnace temperatures.

NASA had long considered a follow-up to the shuttle program, but the perennially cash-strapped agency cancelled those plans a few months ago and instead was preparing to upgrade and refurbish the existing orbiters, hoping to make them last until 2020. Instead of a shuttle replacement, NASA decided to spend $2.4 billion to develop an Orbital Space Plane that would carry astronauts to the International Space Station and serve as a space lifeboat. The job of conducting science missions and ferrying cargo would have been left to the aging shuttle fleet.

Undoubtedly, those plans will now change. Dr. Harrison Schmitt, geologist and Apollo 17 astronaut, told Space.com: "I suspect this tragedy will add new impetus to the Orbital Space Plane, more than likely changing its direction to become not just a rescue vehicle but also a vehicle for access to space."

Shortly after the Challenger disaster in 1986, Dr. Sally Ride, America's first woman in space, wrote a paper entitled "Leadership and America's Future in Space" in which she detailed the need for the country to reassert its role as the world's leading spacefaring nation. As the paper noted, "Leadership cannot simply be proclaimed — it must be earned. As NASA evaluates its goals and objectives within the framework of National Space Policy, the agency must first understand what is required to 'maintain U.S. space leadership,' since that understanding will direct the selection of national objectives."

Dr. Ride's report called for certain steps that would reestablish the country's leadership role in space: a "Mission to Planet Earth" program that would study our planet from orbit; the continuing exploration of the Solar System with robotic probes; the establishment of a permanent scientific outpost on the moon; and an eventual manned landing on Mars.

In the intervening years, the first two of those objectives have been met, but America is no closer to returning to the moon or a Mars landing than we were when the report was written. Some say NASA has lost its vision, delaying outward expansion through the Solar System in favor of near-Earth-orbit missions such as the Columbia's, which advance scientific knowledge but continue to travel the same trail blazed by many previous spacecraft. If America is to regain her role of space leadership and truly explore the unknown, it is obvious an entirely new generation of spacecraft will be needed.

Gregory Benford, University of California professor of physics and astronomy and noted science fiction author, says that NASA now stands at a crossroads: "This is an historic moment, one of great opportunity. NASA can either rise to the challenge and scrap the shuttle, or just muddle along. An intermediate path would use the shuttles on a reduced schedule, while developing a big booster capable of hauling up the big loads needed to build more onto the station. This would be cost-effective and smart."

In the near term, there are still three astronauts orbiting Earth every 90 minutes or so aboard the International Space Station. Astronauts Ken Bowersox and Donald Pettit and Cosmonaut Nikolai Budarin, collectively called Expedition 6, were scheduled to come home in March 2003. There is a Russian Soyuz vehicle docked at the station which could bring the three back any time, but the crew has enough food and supplies to stay in orbit until June. With the shuttle fleet grounded, ISS Mission Control is debating an early Soyuz mission to swap out the crew and keep the space outpost staffed until shuttle flights can resume.

This was to be a peak year for space station construction, with 10 shuttle flights to the orbital outpost scheduled. Components of the station's backbone, a truss that supports the solar arrays and houses cooling mechanisms, would have been added to extend it from its current length of 134 feet to 310 feet, nearly tripling the length of the ISS. Now all construction will halt until the shuttle flies again.

The long-term implications of the Columbia's death are even murkier. It is hoped the tragedy will not affect NASA's ability to launch unmanned probes to Mars and the outer Solar System, especially if its budget is increased in the wake of the accident. Two identical Martian Rovers are scheduled for launch in 2003, with much more range than the small Pathfinder rover that explored a tiny area of the planet in 1997. Each of the upgraded vehicles will be able to cover about 110 yards of Martian landscape per day, and unlike the short-lived Pathfinder, they're built to last for a year or more.

Further out, NASA has plans to send a succession of robotic spacecraft to the Red Planet in the next few years. In 2005, the agency plans to launch a powerful scientific craft, the Mars Reconnaissance Orbiter, which will look for water on the planet and survey Mars close-up at an amazing resolution of 8 to 12 inches — great enough to spot a Martian basketball on the surface if one existed. Its followup is planned to be a roving science laboratory with even greater capabilities than the twin 2003 rovers, followed by small "scout" missions which might involve aerial vehicles. Around 2014, NASA would like to launch a spacecraft that would scoop up some Martian dirt and return it to Earth.

Already on the drawing boards is a next-generation nuclear propulsion system called Prometheus, which would provide a much faster trip to the outer planets. A project called the Jupiter Icy Moons Tour would test the technology, zipping around the Jovian system while sending back photos and data of the giant planet.

Because Prometheus would make it possible to get to Mars in only two months instead of the six months it takes with traditional rockets, there has been speculation that a nuclear engine could make human spaceflight to Mars a possibility long before previously thought. But in the wake of the Columbia disaster, Mars seems farther away than ever.

And yet, as Benford put it, "A Mars expedition would be the grandest exploit open to the 21st Century. It would take about 2.5 years, every day closely monitored by a huge Earthside audience and fraught with peril.

"This is what we should be doing. Such an adventure would resonate with a world beset by wars and woes. It has a grandeur appropriate to the advanced nations, who should do it together.

"The first step will be getting away from the poor, clunky shuttle, a beast designed 30 years ago and visibly failing now. How we respond to the challenge of this failure will tell the tale for decades to come, and may become a marking metaphor for the entire century."

Benford, a long-time NASA advisor, notes that the International Space Station has been touted as a waystation, a jumping-off point for missions to Mars and the rest of the Solar System. But before that can happen, he says, two new technologies must be in place: "First, development of a true closed biosphere in low or zero gravity. The station recycles only urine; otherwise, it is camping in space, not truly living there.

"Second, we must develop centrifugal gravity. Decades of trials show clearly that zero. g is very bad for us. The Russians who set the endurance records in space have never fully recovered. Going to Mars demands that crews arrive after the half year journey able to walk, at least. No crew returning from space after half a year ever have, even for weeks afterward. So we must get more data, between one gravity and none. Mars has 0.38 g; how will we perform there? Nobody knows.

"Spinning a habitat at the other end of a cable, counter-balanced by a dead mass like a missile upper stage, is the obvious first way to try intermediate gravities. The International Space Station has tried very few innovations, and certainly nothing as fruitful as a centrifugal experiment. Until a livelier spirit animates the official space program, the tough jobs of getting into orbit cheaply, and living there self sufficiently, will probably have to be done by private interests who can angle a profit from it. But not right away."

Still, there is no doubt humans will someday explore our Solar System and then beyond. Images from the Voyager and Galileo space probes have given us tantalizing images of erupting volcanoes on distant moons and frozen seas where life may have arisen and may still survive beneath the ice. Places that were once just points of light in a telescope are now revealed as worlds in their own right, keeping secrets yet to be discovered. Although we've barely dipped our toe in the ocean of space, those small ripples are expanding ever outward, and we'll someday follow them to those new worlds, and eventually the stars.

As he paused to contemplate the cosmos

during a moonwalk near Hadley Rille on Apollo 15, astronaut David Scott summed it all up: "As I stand out here in the wonders of the unknown at Hadley, I sort of realize there's a fundamental truth to our nature. Man must explore. And this is exploration at its greatest."

Appendix I
Shuttle and Space Web Resources

Space.com
http://www.space.com
Up-to-the-minute news on the Columbia investigation, as well as the latest information about planned launches, space probes and astronomy.

MSNBC Space News
http://www.msnbc.com/news/spacenews_front.asp?cp1=1
Extensive page of information, including crew biographies, an overview of the shuttle fleet and many images and videos.

CNN Space Page
http://www.cnn.com/TECH/space
Shuttle news, Space Chronicles, feedback page and video.

NASA Human Spaceflight
http://spaceflight.nasa.gov
All the latest breaking news from NASA, including status reports, press briefings and a link to the Columbia investigation page. You can also read letters from the STS-107 families and record your condolences online.

Spaceflight Now
http://www.spaceflightnow.com/index.html
In-depth coverage of Columbia's mission and the investigation, including a timeline of her final re-entry. A news archive is included, and a NewsAlert email newsletter is offered which can be delivered to your desktop.

NASA Watch
http://www.reston.com/nasa/shuttle.news.html
A non-NASA site dedicated to providing third-party information about the agency. Their motto: "Remember: It's YOUR space agency. Get involved. Take it back. Make it work — for YOU."

Kennedy Space Center
http://www.ksc.nasa.gov
The official KSC Web page, featuring Columbia news plus the latest goings-on at the Center.

Heavens Above
http://www.heavens-above.com
You can use information from this site to find out when the International Space Station or other satellite will be visible from your area.

Air and Space Magazine
http://www.airspacemag.com
Web home of the Smithsonian Institution's aerospace publication from the National Air and

Space Museum. Article reprints are included, as well as subscription information.

Jet Propulsion Laboratory
http://www.jpl.nasa.gov
News from the world of robotic space exploration.

Alien Passages
http://www.alienpassages.com/shuttle.htm
Science fiction-oriented site with shuttle news.

Liftoff To Space Exploration
http://liftoff.msfc.nasa.gov
NASA educational site for teenagers, focusing on types of rockets, living in space, fundamentals of space travel and other information for young people.

NASA Kids
http://kids.msfc.nasa.gov
Web site for the under-13 set, including games, basic space information and articles by other children.

Appendix II
American Manned Space Program Timeline

PROJECT MERCURY
Freedom 7 — Alan Shepard — May 5, 1961
Liberty Bell 7 — Virgil "Gus" Grissom — July 21, 1961
Friendship 7 — John Glenn — Feb. 20, 1962
Aurora 7 — Scott Carpenter — May 24, 1962
Sigma 7 — Walter "Wally" Schirra — Oct. 3, 1962
Faith 7 — Gordon Cooper — May 15-16, 1963

PROJECT GEMINI
Gemini 3 — Gus Grissom, John Young — March 23, 1965
Gemini 4 — James McDivitt, Edward White — June 3-7, 1965
Gemini 5 — Gordon Cooper, Charles "Pete" Conrad — Aug. 21-29, 1965
Gemini 7 — Frank Borman, James Lovell — Dec. 4-18, 1965
Gemini 6A — Wally Schirra, Thomas Stafford — Dec. 15-16, 1965
Gemini 8 — Neil Armstrong, David Scott — March 16, 1966

Gemini 9A — Thomas Stafford, Eugene Cernan — June 3-6, 1966

Gemini 10 — John Young, Michael Collins — July 18-21, 1966

Gemini 11 — Pete Conrad, Richard Gordon — Sept. 12-15, 1966

Gemini 12 — James Lovell, Edwin "Buzz" Aldrin — Nov. 11-15, 1966

PROJECT APOLLO — SATURN I

Apollo 7 — Wally Schirra, Donn Eisele, Walter Cunningham — Oct. 11-22, 1968

PROJECT APOLLO — SATURN V

Apollo 8 — Frank Borman, James Lovell, William Anders — Dec. 21-27, 1968

Apollo 9 — James McDivitt, David Scott, Russell "Rusty" Schweickart — March 3-13, 1969

Apollo 10 — Thomas Stafford, John Young, Gene Cernan — May 18-26, 1969

Apollo 11 — Neil Armstrong, Michael Collins, Buzz Aldrin — July 16-24, 1969

Apollo 12 — Pete Conrad, Richard Gordon, Alan Bean — Nov. 14-24, 1969

Apollo 13 — James Lovell, Jack Swigert, Fred Haise — April 11-17, 1970

Apollo 14 — Alan Shepard, Stuart Roosa, Edgar Mitchell — Jan. 31-Feb. 9, 1971

Apollo 15 — David Scott, Al Worden, James Irwin — July 26-Aug. 7, 1971

Apollo 16 — John Young, Thomas Mattingly, Charles Duke, Jr. — April 16-27, 1972

Apollo 17 — Gene Cernan, Ron Evans, Harrison Schmitt — Dec. 7-19, 1972

APOLLO-SOYUZ TEST PROJECT — SATURN IB
Thomas Stafford, Vance Brand, Donald "Deke" Slayton — July 15-24, 1975

SPACE SHUTTLE — NOTABLE FLIGHTS

1981: STS-1 — First flight of the space shuttle (Columbia)

1982: STS-5 — First commercial satellite deployment, with two released (Columbia)

1983: STS-6 — First spacewalk from shuttle, lasting 4 hours, 10 minutes (Challenger)

STS-7 — Sally Ride becomes first American woman in space (Challenger)

STS-9 — First Spacelab mission. First non-U.S. astronaut, Germany's Ulf Merbold (Columbia)

1984: 41-B — First non-tethered spacewalk, taken by Bruce McCandless in MMU (Challenger)

41-C — First satellite repair in space (Challenger)

1986: 51-L — Challenger explosion

1989: STS-30 — Magellan spacecraft deployed on a successful mission to Venus (Atlantis)

STS-34 — Galileo spacecraft deployed on successful mission to Jupiter (Atlantis)

1990: STS-31 — Launch of Hubble Space Telescope (Discovery)

1991: STS-37 — Gamma Ray Observatory deployed (Atlantis)

STS-40 — First Spacelab scientific mission (Columbia)

1992: STS-47 — May C. Jemison becomes first African-American woman in space (Endeavor)

1993: STS-61 — First Hubble servicing mission to correct faulty optics (Endeavor)

1994: STS-60 — First Russian cosmonaut on a U.S. space shuttle (Discovery)

1995: STS-71 — First Shuttle/Mir docking. One hundredth U.S. human space launch (Atlantis)

1998: STS-95 — John Glenn, first American to orbit Earth, flies again at the age of 77 (Discovery)

STS-88 — First International Space Station assembly mission (Endeavor)

2000: STS-92 — One hundredth shuttle mission (Discovery)

2003: STS-107 — Columbia is lost

Appendix III
Wall of Remembrance

The United States space program has lost many of its best and brightest over the years. Following is a complete list of astronauts who have perished.

Name	Program/Flight	DOD-Cause of death
MERCURY THROUGH SKYLAB		
Charles Basset	Gemini program (No flights)	2/28/66-Training mission plane crash
Roger Chaffee	Apollo 1	1/27/67-Apollo 1 fire
Pete Conrad	Gemini 5 & 6, Apollo 12, Skylab 2	7/7/99-Motorcycle accident
Donn Eisele	Apollo 7	12/2/87-Heart attack
Ronald Evans	Apollo 17	4/6/90-Heart attack
Theodore Freeman	Gemini program (No flights)	10/31/64-Training mission plane crash
Edward Givens	Apollo program (No flights)	6/6/67-Automobile accident
Virgil 'Gus' Grissom	Mercury 4, Gemini 3, Apollo 1	1/27/67-Apollo 1 fire

Jim Irwin	Apollo 15	8/8/91-Heart attack
Stuart Roosa	Apollo 14	12/12/94-Pancreatitis
Alan Shepherd	Mercury 3, Apollo 14	7/21/98-Leukemia
Donald 'Deke' Slayton	Mercury program (No flights), Apollo-Soyuz	6/13/93-Brain tumor
Elliot See	Gemini program (No flights)	2/28/66-Training mission plane crash
John Swigert	Apollo 13	12/27/82-Cancer
Edward White	Gemini 4, Apollo 1	1/27/67-Apollo 1 fire
Clifton Williams	Gemini program (No flights)	10/5/67-Training mission plane crash

SPACE SHUTTLE

Michael Anderson	2/1/03-Columbia explosion
David Brown	2/1/03-Columbia explosion
"Sonny" Carter	4/5/91-Commercial plane crash
Kalpana Chalwa	2/1/03-Columbia explosion
Lauren Clark	2/1/03-Columbia explosion
David Griggs	6/17/89-Training mission plane crash

Karl Henize	10/5/93-Heart attack climbing Mt. Everest
Rick Husband	2/1/03-Columbia explosion
William McCool	2/1/03-Columbia explosion
Ronald McNair	1/28/86-Challenger explosion
Ellison Onizuka	1/28/86-Challenger explosion
Robert Overmyer	3/22/86-Test aircraft crash
Judith Resnik	1/28/86-Challenger explosion
Francis Scobee	1/28/86-Challenger explosion
Michael Smith	1/28/86-Challenger explosion
Stephen Thorne	5/24/86-Private plane crash
Charles Veach	10/3/93-Prolonged illness
David Walker	4/23/01-Cancer

INTERNATIONAL SPACE STATION

Patricia Robertson	5/24/01-Private plane crash

Acknowledgments

The authors would like to acknowledge the contributions of the following people: Their wives, Maryanne Cantrell and Nanette Vaughan, for their unwavering love and understanding; Ceri Usmar for her unflagging enthusiasm and meticulous eye for detail; and Tony Seidl, who made this project possible.